DIANA PANKE,
LUKAS GRUNDSFELD, AND
PAWEL TVERSKOI

EXIT THREATS IN REGIONAL INTERNATIONAL ORGANIZATIONS

First published in Great Britain in 2025 by

Bristol University Press
University of Bristol
1–9 Old Park Hill
Bristol
BS2 8BB
UK
t: +44 (0)117 374 6645
e: bup-info@bristol.ac.uk

Details of international sales and distribution partners are available at
bristoluniversitypress.co.uk

© Diana Panke, Lukas Grundsfeld, and Pawel Tverskoi 2025

The digital PDF version of this title is available open access and distributed under the terms of the Creative Commons Attribution-NonCommercial-NoDerivatives 4.0 International licence (https://creativecommons.org/licenses/by-nc-nd/4.0/) which permits reproduction and distribution for non-commercial use without further permission provided the original work is attributed.

https://doi.org/10.51952/9781529255799

British Library Cataloguing in Publication Data
A catalogue record for this book is available from the British Library

ISBN 978-1-5292-5577-5 paperback
ISBN 978-1-5292-5578-2 ePub
ISBN 978-1-5292-5579-9 OA PDF

The right of Diana Panke, Lukas Grundsfeld, and Pawel Tverskoi to be identified as authors of this work has been asserted by them in accordance with the Copyright, Designs and Patents Act 1988.

All rights reserved: no part of this publication may be reproduced, stored in a retrieval system, or transmitted in any form or by any means, electronic, mechanical, photocopying, recording, or otherwise without the prior permission of Bristol University Press.

Every reasonable effort has been made to obtain permission to reproduce copyrighted material. If, however, anyone knows of an oversight, please contact the publisher.

The statements and opinions contained within this publication are solely those of the authors and not of the University of Bristol or Bristol University Press. The University of Bristol and Bristol University Press disclaim responsibility for any injury to persons or property resulting from any material published in this publication.

Bristol University Press works to counter discrimination on
grounds of gender, race, disability, age and sexuality.

Cover design: blu inc
Front cover image: Shutterstock/Ariya J

Contents

List of Figures and Tables		iv
List of Abbreviations		v
Preface and Acknowledgments		ix
one	Introduction	1
two	Regional International Organizations: Member State Dissatisfaction in Community Organizations	16
three	Exit Threats as Severe Contestations	28
four	A Systems Theory Perspective on the Prevalence of Exit Threats	43
five	Empirical Analysis: Accounting for the Varying Prevalence of Exit Threats	58
six	Conclusions	93
Notes		107
Appendix		114
References		129
Index		162

List of Figures and Tables

Figures

3.1	Exit threats by country (1945–2022)	39
3.2	Exit threats experienced by RIO (1945–2022)	40
3.3	Exit threats issued over time (cumulative for all RIOs)	41
4.1	A systems theory perspective on exit threats	45

Tables

4.1	Overview of hypotheses	55
5.1	Rare event regressions (controls omitted)	65
5.2	Rare event regressions (controls shown)	89
A.1	List of RIOs	114
A.2	Newspaper coverage of RIOs	118
A.3	Summary statistics	123
A.4	Correlation matrix	124
A.5	Robustness check multilevel regressions	126
A.6	Robustness check with security and economic competencies	128

List of Abbreviations

AC	Arctic Council
ACC	Arab Cooperation Council
ACD	Asia Cooperation Dialogue
ACS	Association of Caribbean States
ACTO	Amazonian Cooperation Treaty Organization
ALADI	Latin American Integration Association
ALBA	Bolivarian Alliance for the Peoples of Our Americas
AMU	Arab Maghreb Union
ANDEAN	Andean Community
APEC	Asia-Pacific Economic Cooperation
ASEAN	Association of Southeast Asian Nations
AU	African Union
BEU	Benelux Economic Union
BIMSTEC	Bay of Bengal Initiative for Multi-Sectoral Technical and Economic Cooperation
BRICS	Brazil, Russia, India, China and South Africa
BSEC	Black Sea Economic Cooperation
CACJ	Central American Court of Justice
CACM	Central American Common Market
CAEU	Council of Arab Economic Unity
CAREC	Central Asia Regional Economic Cooperation
CARICOM	Caribbean Community
CCTS	Cooperation Council of Turkic Speaking States
CE	Conseil de l'Entente
CEEAC	Communauté Economique des États de l'Afrique Centrale
CEFTA	Central European Free Trade Agreement
CEI	Central European Initiative
CELAC	Community of Latin American and Caribbean States

CEMAC	Communauté économique et monétaire de l'Afrique centrale
CENSAD	Community of Sahel-Saharan States
CEPGL	Economic Community of the Great Lakes Countries
CICA	Conference on Interaction and Confidence Building Measures in Asia
CIS	Commonwealth of Independent States
CoE	Council of Europe
COMESA	Common Market for Eastern and Southern Africa
COW	Correlates of War
CSTO	Collective Security Treaty (Organization)
DPI	Database of Political Institutions
EAC	East African Community
EAEU	Eurasian Economic Union
ECHR	European Court of Human Rights
ECO	Economic Cooperation Organization
ECOWAS	Economic Community of West African States
EFTA	European Free Trade Association
G20	Group of 20
G5S	G5 Sahel
GCC	Gulf Cooperation Council
GDP	Gross Domestic Product
GGC	Gulf of Guinea Commission
GUAM	Organization for Democracy and Economic Development
IACHR	Inter-American Commission on Human Rights
ICGLR	International Conference on the Great Lakes Region
IGAD	Intergovernmental Authority on Development
IGO	International Governmental Organization
ILO	International Labour Organization
IO	International Organization
IOC	Indian Ocean Commission

LIST OF ABBREVIATIONS

IORA	Indian Ocean Rim Association
LAS	League of Arab States
LCBC	Lake Chad Basin Commission
LIO	Liberal International Order
MERCOSUR	Mercado Comun del Sur
MGC	Mekong-Ganga Cooperation
MRU	Mano River Union
MSG	Melanesian Spearhead Group
NAFTA	North American Free Trade Organization
NATO	North Atlantic Treaty Organization
NC	Nordic Council
OAS	Organization of American States
OAU	Organization of African Unity
ODECA	Organization of Central American States
OECS	Organisation of Eastern Caribbean States
ODIHR	Office for Democratic Institutions and Human Rights
OSCE	Organisation for Security and Co-operation in Europe
P5	Permanent Five United Nations Security Council Members
PACE	Parliamentary Assembly of the Council of Europe
PIF	Pacific Islands Forum
RIO	Regional International Organization
ROCO	Regional Organizations Competencies Dataset
SAARC	South Asian Association for Regional Cooperation
SACU	Southern African Customs Union
SADC	Southern African Development Community
SADCC	Southern African Development Co-ordination Conference
SCO	Shanghai Cooperation Organization
SEATO	Southeast Asia Treaty Organization
SELA	Latin American Economic System
SICA	Central American Integration System

SPC	Pacific Community
UEMOA	West African Economic and Monetary Union
UNASUR	Union of South American Nations
UNGA	United Nations General Assembly
WEU	Western European Union
WTO	Warsaw Treaty Organisation

Preface and Acknowledgments

The book *Exit Threats in Regional International Organizations* addresses a topic of great interest to us, namely the contestation of regional international organizations (RIOs) by their own member states. Exit threats are a special and severe form of contestation as they not only publicly showcase internal dissent but carry the potential to seriously harm the organization in question. Thus, we are happy to contribute with this book to the large and growing literatures on contestation beyond the nation state as well as on comparative international organization research and comparative regionalism.

This book is part of the research project 'Should I stay or should I go? State Exits from Regional Organizations', funded by the German Research Foundation (DFG; PA 1257/10–1). We are grateful for the financial support, which was crucial for the creation of the exit threat dataset as well as the qualitative analysis, especially the interviews with RIO and member state officials. Also, we are grateful to all interviewees: without them and their generous dedication of time to answer our questions, the insights on exit threats and underlying dynamics would have remained superficial.

We also thank Christina Augustin, Léonie Berton, Antonia Damm, Christina Görisch, Rouven Harms, Lisa Hartmann, Luise Hartmann, Luise Kienel, Dagmar Kohlmeier, Fenna Kreuz, Hanne Oldenhof, Moritz Pohlner, Tim Rauschenberger, Tobias Sauer, Mirjam Schellinger, Martin Stoll, Maarten van Melis, Tim Vent, Chira Walke, and Lukas Weißenberger for research support, including, but not limited to, the transcription of interviews and literature management. Moreover, we would like to thank Barbara Gumbert from the University of Freiburg as well as Annika Jost from Freie Universität Berlin for excellent project administration!

As always, it was a pleasure working with Bristol University Press and we are grateful to Stephen Wenham, Izzie Green, Zoë Forbes and the entire BUP team for excellent editorial support.

For helpful comments on our exit project in general and the exit threat research in particular, we would like to thank Tanja Börzel, Ljiljana Biukovic, Eugénia da Conceição-Heldt, Benjamin Daßler, Cecilia Ducci, Mette Eilstrup-Sangiovanni, Elaine Fahey, Benjamin Faude, Orfeo Fioretos, Yoram Haftel, Tim Heinkelmann-Wild, Mirko Heinzel, Randall Henning, Andreas Hofmann, Simon Koschut, Alexander Libman, Andrea Liese, Flavia Lucenti, Alex Onatunji, Bernhard Reinsberg, Andrea Ribeiro Hoffmann, Federico Salvati, Duncan Snidal, Fred Söderbaum, and Matthew Stephen. A special thank you goes to Tainá Estanislau Siman and Sören Stapel, who read through the very final version of the book.

ONE

Introduction

Presidents Hugo Chavez of Venezuela and Evo Morales of Bolivia have warned they might pull their countries from the five-nation group [Andean Community] if the other members Colombia, Peru and Ecuador ratify trade pacts with the United States.
> API, 'Peru's President Asks Venezuela, Bolivia to Consider Withdrawal from Trade Bloc', 2006

Prime Minister David Cameron warned on Wednesday that unless the European Union reforms to tackle the problems at its heart, Britain risked drifting towards an exit.
> AFP, 'Without EU Reform, Risk of British Exit: Cameron', 2013

The Burundian government is examining whether it should stay in the East African Community. Burundi and Tanzania are often put aside in the works of the EAC. Tanzania has threatened to withdraw from the community. On its part, Burundi has declared that the issue is being analysed.
> BBC, 'Burundi Threatens to Withdraw from Regional Body for Exclusion', 2013a

> Someone said, '[...] would you leave us if we don't pay our bills?' They hated my answer. I said, 'Yeah, I would consider it.'
>
> Donald Trump, cited by Atlantic Council, 'Trump Confirms He Threatened to Withdraw from NATO', 2018

The above quotations are but a few examples indicative of perennial contestations faced by regional international organizations (RIOs).[1] Over time, more than 70 RIOs have been created in Africa, the Americas, Asia, and Europe, often expanding in membership size as well as scope of policy competencies, and thereby indicating that regional governance has become more widespread and increasingly important for the states concerned (Acharya and Johnston 2007, Börzel et al 2012a, Vinokurov and Libman 2017, Panke and Stapel 2018). This is furthered by the notion that, due to the geography-related membership criterion, RIOs tend to be more homogenous than global IOs. Thus, member states often have historical and cultural experiences in common, face similar socio-economic conditions and often also similar geographic as well as climatic challenges, which foster identity building and the notion of RIOs as 'community organizations' (Slocum and van Langenhove 2005, Thomas 2017, Spandler 2019).

Yet, as the opening quotations indicate, despite being considered community organizations, RIOs are not uncontested. On the contrary. This book shows that member states sooner or later experience situations when they are dissatisfied with a RIO – and thus have reasons to challenge a specific RIO. This is the case for states that are small or large, economically strong or weak, democratic or autocratic, as well as for states that have been members of a RIO for a long time, or that had joined only recently. This book sheds light on one specific form of contestation: exit threats. It examines how prevalent the phenomenon of exit threats is and explains why some states voice more and why some RIOs receive more exit threats than others. Consequently, the book addresses the following research question: Why does the prevalence of exit threats differ between and within RIOs?

Shedding light on exit threats and accounting for the observed variation is important, as such threats are a severe form of member state contestation, publicly putting into question the legitimacy and utility of a RIO as such. Exit threats are public statements by state officials indicating the state's intention to terminate its membership in an organization (see also von Borzyskowski and Vabulas 2023). Thus, in contrast to a notification of withdrawal, which is a matter-of-fact statement of a state's already taken decision (for example, Austria from the Central European Initiative (CEI), see Panke et al 2024), an exit threat is an expression of dissatisfaction with a RIO linked to the possibility of terminating its membership in the future. Exit threats represent challenges for RIOs as they can set the path on a slippery slope toward actual withdrawals, and, short thereof, also damage trust and confidence in the organization by questioning its value as an outlet for institutionalized cooperation as such. For instance, President Trump's threat to withdraw from NATO in 2018, mentioned in the opening quotes above, publicly showcased the existence of RIO-internal cleavages and signaled a member state's reduced commitment to future multilateral cooperation in this very organization (Schuette 2021). This jeopardized the deterrence function of NATO and would have severely harmed the functioning and purpose of the organization in the future, had the exit threat not been swiftly addressed internally (Dijkstra et al 2024, Dijkstra et al 2025). Therefore, threats to withdraw carry significant implications for (dis)integration of the affected organizations and the effectiveness of governance beyond the nation state (Sampson 2017, Leruth et al 2019, Rosamond 2019, Panke et al 2024, von Borzyskowski and Vabulas 2024b).

Despite being community organizations, member states can encounter situations in which they are dissatisfied with a RIO and articulate this in the form of public criticism.[2] Moreover, grievances can also be articulated in the form of exit threats, as the above examples from the US and the North Atlantic Treaty Organization (NATO), the UK and the European Union (EU), Venezuela and ANDEAN as well as Burundi and the EAC illustrate. In fact, a comprehensive analysis of 73 RIOs over an extended period of time (1945–2022) illustrates that 123 exit threats were voiced over this timespan and that their prevalence differed between and within RIOs. In total, 65 different states made threats to withdraw from RIOs, among them Morocco and Russia (six each), the UK and Venezuela (four each), and Kiribati and Nigeria (two each). While the African Union (AU) and the Pacific Islands Forum (PIF) received the most exit threats, the Caribbean Community (CARICOM), the International Conference on the Great Lakes Region (ICGLR), the Intergovernmental Authority on Development (IGAD), and the Central American Integration System (SICA) are among the RIOs that were only subject to one withdrawal threat each. The observed variation is puzzling: it is not the case that only big or only small or only longstanding or recently admitted member states articulate their respective perceptions of discontent with RIO policies or (in)activities via exit threats, and it is also not the case that recently established organizations or RIOs from a particular geographic region are especially subject to withdrawal threats. But why are some states more inclined to issue threats to end their membership in RIOs and why does this happen more frequently in some organizations compared to others?

Summary of the argument

States form international organizations (IOs) in order to cooperate in institutionalized settings. There are different types of IOs such as global and regional IOs, rule-setting/standard-setting versus activity-centered/operational IOs, democratic versus autocratic IOs or China-led versus US-led

IOs, to name but a few. Due to the high number of different IO types, most IO studies are usually selective in terms of which type they focus on. This book follows suit and empirically studies regional international organizations (RIOs), whose membership criteria is geography-based – unlike global IOs, which all sovereign states can potentially join. RIOs are often regarded as community organizations in which the members pursue common goals or address problems, which often have a regional scale. Over time, 73 RIOs have been created, of which the EU, the Organization of American States (OAS), the Economic Community of West African States (ECOWAS), and the Association of Southeast Asian Nations (ASEAN) are just four prominent examples. Often, RIOs increased in membership size as well as the scope of policy competencies covered in their treaties and other primary law. Taken together, this indicates that regional governance became increasingly important across the world.

Yet, RIOs are not uncontested – on the contrary. This book illustrates that small and large, old and new as well as rich and poorer states sooner or later experience situations in which they are dissatisfied with a RIO they are members of and have therefore grounds to contest the RIO in question. This book focuses on the prevalence of one specific form of contestation: exit threats. Threats to withdraw are a severe form of contestation, publicly putting into question the legitimacy and value of a RIO as such, thereby undermining the organization. This was evident, for example in Donald Trump's threat in 2018 to withdraw from NATO, which triggered shock waves among the fellow NATO member states. Thus, exit threats carry significant implications for the internal functioning and legitimacy of RIOs as well as their external effectiveness.

However, while many states have grievances with RIOs, not all of them issue exit threats. In other words, member state dissatisfaction is a necessary – but not sufficient – condition for RIO contestations through exit threats voiced by member states. This short book is the first to provide systematic insights into the prevalence of exit threats between and within RIOs. Based on a novel dataset, we identify 123 instances of exit threats between 1945 and 2022. This book studies why some states are more prone to voice exit threats and why RIOs differ to the extent to which they are contested by such threats.

The book's research question is answered in a theory-guided empirical manner, in which we combine rare event logit regressions with qualitative analysis in the form of narrative evidence. Theoretically, we draw on Easton's systems theory as this approach allows us to capture specific support, which is influence-based, as well as diffuse support, which is legitimacy-based, as drivers behind the variation in the prevalence of exit threats. We identify factors impacting states' ability to address grievances by influencing the organization's policy output (specific support) as well as states' general commitment to institutionalized cooperation (diffuse support).

Examining the plausibility of the hypotheses based on a set of 73 RIOs, the book makes two arguments. First, exit threats are more prevalent the fewer chances states have to influence RIOs' throughput processes and to transform demands into outputs due to lacking power and ideological dissimilarity, which is furthered by the presence of majority voting rules and a broad set of policy competencies of the organization in question. Also, specific support is more limited when states are weak or ideologically dissimilar from the other member states, as this reduces their chances to influence RIO outputs. Second, compared to influence-based specific support, legitimacy-based diffuse support plays a minor role. States are only more likely to issue exit threats when their overall commitment toward the RIO is low due to the absence of domestic democratic socialization.

The book's findings contribute to the research on international contestations, resilience of RIOs as well as comparative (R)IO research and comparative regionalism. The book is also extremely timely. With the 2024 US elections,

Donald Trump, who in the past has often been dissatisfied with RIOs in which the US is a member, including the North Atlantic Free Trade Agreement (NAFTA) and NATO, and who is not attributing much diffuse support to RIOs, new exit threat contestations of such organizations can be expected. Broadly speaking, the rise of nationalism and populism in many countries in the Global North and the Global South is likely to trigger dissatisfaction with institutionalized regional international cooperation. Such dissatisfaction is likely to be articulated by exit threats in those RIOs in which ideological differences between member states become heightened, in turn reducing the chances to exert influence in the throughput process. Such limitations in specific support are particularly problematic in situations in which diffuse support is also in short supply due to lacking democratic socialization.

Chapter outline

To answer the research question 'Why does the prevalence of exit threats differ between and within RIOs?', the book is organized into six chapters. Chapter Two first provides an overview of different IO types and presents the rationale for why this book empirically studies RIOs as one specific type. It goes on to outline that although RIOs tend to be smaller and more homogenous than global IOs and are therefore often considered as being 'community organizations', member states nevertheless experience an array of grievances concerning a broad set of policies and RIO (in)activities,[3] which can be expressed in the form of exit threats. While a systematic overview of instances of dissatisfaction of the more than 190 member states of more than 70 RIOs in the period from 1945 to 2022 is beyond the scope of this book, we draw on secondary literature and a media analysis to illustrate with narrative evidence that member states' dissatisfaction with RIOs is widespread – both across states, that is large and small, old and new members, and organizations, including from all regions, established and recent RIOs, larger and smaller ones. Hence, sooner or later all states encounter situations in which the necessary, but not sufficient, condition for exit threats is present.

State dissatisfaction can be expressed with exit threats against the respective organization. Accordingly, in Chapter Three, the book provides an overview of the prevalence of exit threats and outlines their variation. In this regard, we draw on the Regional Organizations' Competencies (ROCO) 2.0 dataset (based on Panke et al 2020), which we extend to include the years 2021 and 2022, covering 73 RIOs in Africa, the Americas, Asia, and Europe between 1945 and 2022. This allows us to investigate a complete sample of one subtype of IOs. This reveals that exit threats were articulated most frequently in the AU and PIF, with more than ten such instances, while other RIOs were less frequently severely contested, such as the CARICOM, ICGLR, IGAD, SICA, the Union of South American Nations (UNASUR), and the Warsaw Treaty Organization (WTO), with one threat of a member state to withdraw from the organization each. Next to the variation among RIOs, the propensity of issuing exit threats also varies among states. 123 exit threats were voiced by 65 states, which differed in the number of threats made. At one end of the spectrum, Morocco and Russia issued exit threats in six instances, while at the other end, several states each threatened just once to withdraw from a RIO, such as Bolivia in ANDEAN in 2006, Eswatini in COMESA in 1997, Bahrain in the Gulf Cooperation Council (GCC) in 1999, and Kazakhstan in the OSCE in 2006.

To derive potential explanations for variation in the prevalence of exit threats in and between RIOs, in Chapter Four we draw on Easton's systems theory (1965). Developed as an analytical framework to explain the persistence of political systems, it is sufficiently abstract to be applicable to all types of IOs, including RIOs. As states' demands towards IOs, IOs' outputs, and states' evaluation of these are indeterminate and idiosyncratic, we focus on factors influencing states' specific and diffuse support for the IO as a political system. Whereas the former refers to states' ability to generally influence the IOs' throughput process, that is the conversion of demands into outputs, the latter captures factors determining states' normative commitment vis-à-vis organizations. Although both types of generalized support are essential for the persistence of political systems, decreases in specific and diffuse support for an IO elevate the chances for exit threats to occur. Based on this line of reasoning, we develop two hypotheses on specific and on diffuse support, which focus on country as well as organizational features to account for variation in a state's general ability to address its dissatisfaction by influencing IO policy outputs (specific support) as well as a state's general commitment to institutionalized cooperation (diffuse support). We expect that exit threats are increasingly prevalent in IOs and states increasingly revert to exit threats when specific and diffuse support decrease.

Easton's systems theory is abstract in nature and the hypotheses derived from it can be applied to all types of IOs, such as regional and global ones (Acharya and Johnston 2007, Börzel et al 2012a, Söderbaum 2016, Panke et al 2020), rule-setting/standard-setting versus activity-centered/operational IOs (Vinokurov and Libman 2017, Rittberger et al 2019), democratic versus autocratic IOs (Pevehouse 2005, Debre 2021) or China-led versus US-led IOs (Stephen 2021, Heinkelmann-Wild et al 2024a). To empirically examine the plausibility of the expectations, we focus on RIOs.

Chapter Five empirically investigates the hypothesis on country (state power, ideological similarity) as well as institutional design features (consensus rule, narrow policy scope) as drivers of specific support as well as the hypothesis on country (socialization into IO, socialization into cooperation) and organizational features (democratic nature of IO, age of IO) as drivers of diffuse support, to gauge whether decreasing generalized support of member states for a RIO increases the chances of exit threats. To this end, we use rare event logit regression and provide qualitative narrative evidence based on interviews and a media analysis to further illustrate the findings.

This shows that exit threats are more prevalent the fewer chances an individual state has to generally influence RIOs' throughput processes transforming its demands into outputs. Importantly, specific support is generated when a state is generally in a good position to shape RIO outputs according to its own demands due to high level of state power, ideological similarity to the other member states, as well as consensus decision-making rules and a narrow policy scope of the RIO. When specific support of a state towards a RIO is high, the propensity of exit threats decreases even when the state in question encounters a situation in which its grievances cannot be remedied. By contrast, exit threats are more likely when states lack power, are ideologically dissimilar to the other member states, decision-making in the RIO is based on majority rule and when the organization covers a broad set of different policy competencies. In such constellations, a state attributes only limited specific support to a RIO. Hence, when such a state encounters a situation in which its grievances are not mitigated, the chances increase that it threatens the RIO with an exit. In other words, while high specific support plays a crucial role in preventing exit threats from being used as a means of contestation, limited specific support increases the prevalence of exit threats in RIOs.

The empirical analysis further shows that while limited specific support is a crucial driver for exit threats, limited diffuse support plays a minor role in comparison. Only a single factor is systematically influencing the likelihood of exit threats: limited democratic socialization. The less states are socialized into dynamics of alternating winning and losing constellations and the less they are socialized into placing value on cooperation in general, the more limited the diffuse support they are likely to attribute to a RIO they are member of. Consequently, when autocratic states encounter situations in which a specific grievance is not remedied, the chances that they revert to exit threats increase. Conversely, when a democratic member state is faced with an unresolved situation of dissatisfaction with a specific RIO policy or a specific RIO (in)activity, the diffuse support that this state attributes to the RIO in question functions as a buffer, reducing the likelihood that the dissatisfied state resorts to an exit threat.

In sum, this chapter shows that states that encounter a situation of being dissatisfied with a RIO are more likely to use exit threats vis-à-vis this organization; the weaker they are, the greater their ideational dissimilarity to other RIO members is, and the less democratically socialized they are. RIOs are particularly prone to attract withdrawal threats when they allow for majority decision-making and have broad policy scopes. Moreover, specific and diffuse support are not mutually exclusive but can be complementary in nature. Also, in RIOs, not every instance of displeasure is expressed through exit threats since the lack of specific support can be compensated by diffuse support and vice versa. Not least because grounds for discontent are abundant, neither specific support nor diffuse support render the respective other type of generalized support irrelevant.

Chapter Six summarizes the main findings and elaborates on avenues for future research.

This book makes three arguments: first, states threatening to withdraw from institutionalized cooperation represents an important phenomenon in global governance, which carries important implications for the legitimacy and effectiveness of the organizations concerned. Yet, while all states sooner or later encounter instances of dissatisfaction, grievances do not automatically lead to exit threats. Easton's systems theory suggests that specific and diffuse support can buffer individual episodes of dissatisfaction; not from occurring but from turning into serious contestations in the form of exit threats.

Second, this book shows that exit threats are more prevalent the fewer chances states have to influence RIOs' throughput processes and transform demands into outputs due to a lack of power and ideological dissimilarity, which is furthered by the presence of majority voting rules and a broad set of policy competencies of the organization in question.[4] Compared to specific support, diffuse support plays a minor role. States are only more likely to issue exit threats when their general commitment towards the RIO is low due to the absence of domestic democratic socialization.[5] The variation of the prevalence of exit threats between and within RIOs is not monocausal in nature but based on multicausal drivers in the form of mainly specific support as well as one particular feature of diffuse support.

Third, both types of support can function as buffers, preventing a state from acting upon its grievances by articulating exit threats. In other words, specific and to a limited extent diffuse support play essential roles. Yet, both forms of support cannot prevent individual instances of discontent from occurring as even powerful and ideologically similar states might sometimes fail to get what they want in a RIO as the German policy proposals concerning migration in the EU in 2015 (Reiners and Tekin 2020) or the French security-related plans in the mid-2020s in the EU context (Bergmann and Müller 2021) exemplify. However, they prevent that a specific instance of dissatisfaction, once it occurs, necessarily turns into a public, RIO-harming contestation in the form of an exit threat. In other words, by reducing the likelihood of exit threats, specific and to a more limited extent also diffuse support are important for the resilience of RIOs.

In the concluding chapter, we not only summarize the main argument but also point to future avenues for research, reflecting on the conditions under which states act upon their exit threats, and actually terminate their membership of an organization. About one in five exits was preceded by threats to leave the RIO. If threats are effective and threatening states obtain concessions, such as NATO's re-emphasis on the 2 percent GDP military spending target in response to Trump's exit threat, actions are rather unlikely to follow words. In Easton's terms, concessions foster specific support and reduce the likelihood for withdrawal threats to escalate into actual exits. This is also less likely when specific support no longer decreases, as conflicts underlying withdrawal threats have ceased or lost relevance. Finally, changes in the government of the contesting state provide chances to re-evaluate grounds for both specific and diffuse support for the RIO in question.

Taken together, this book speaks to and makes contributions to several debates. This includes scholarship on challenges regional and global international organizations are facing through contestation by their own member states. In this regard, contributions have examined member state contestations through non-compliance (Börzel 2022), critique and blame-shifting (Heinkelmann-Wild et al 2024b), or the contestation of RIOs' democracy norms through coups d'état (Hohlstein 2022). Another strand of research focuses on the dynamics of norm contestation within international institutionalized settings (Wiener 2018, Zimmermann et al 2023). Recent scholarship has examined withdrawals of states from mostly global IOs as one specific form of contestation (Brölmann et al 2018, Shi 2018, von Borzyskowski and Vabulas 2019b, 2022, 2024a, 2025, Choi 2022, Dijkstra and Ghassim 2024). This book is the first to zoom in one specific form of member state contestation, namely exit threats, which – although frequent in global and regional IOs – have received no systematic attention as of yet. While von Borzyskowski and Vabulas (2023) analyze the effectiveness of exit threats in terms of achieving IO reforms, state of the art contestation literature does not yet know which states are most inclined to voice such threats and which RIOs are subject to more such contestations than others – and why. This is surprising, given that exit threat contestations – just as the already well-studied forms of contestation – can trigger severe negative consequences for the contested RIO.

Second, this book contributes to scholarship on international order and the resilience of international order and institutionalized global governance (Fergusson and Zakaria 2017). Research on the resilience and survival of regional and global international organizations in the wake of external crises or internal challenges (Dingwerth et al 2019b, Nolte and Weiffen 2021, Dijkstra et al 2025b), as well as legitimacy crises of international organizations (Dellmuth et al 2022a, Sommerer et al 2022, Dellmuth and Tallberg 2023) has outlined that today's global and regional IOs are under pressure. While the sources of pressure can be internal and external in nature and – as the contestation literature argues – come in different shapes and forms, global IOs and RIOs do neither automatically cease to exist when faced with challenges, nor do they automatically survive. Hence, the above body of literature points out that questions of IO resilience are important. In studying exit threats, this book adds to this body of research by providing insights into which organizational and which member state features are likely to reduce contestations from within or – by consequence – which reforms are likely to make global and regional IOs more resilient, reducing one specific form of internal contestations.

Third, this book also contributes to research on comparative regionalism. This body of scholarship studies RIOs in a comparative perspective (Börzel and Risse 2016). Much of the literature takes stock of the number and purpose of the RIOs created in different regions over time and sheds light on important features, such as their institutional design (Vinokurov and Libman 2017, Panke et al 2020), questions of RIO authority and legitimacy (Hooghe et al 2017, Söderbaum et al 2021), and questions concerning the diffusion of norms and institutional design (Börzel and Van Hüllen 2015, Lenz 2021, Stapel 2022). This book adds to this body of research by examining 73 different RIOs and comparatively studying the exit threat-related challenges they face. The analysis of the prevalence of exit threats between and within RIOs provides novel insights into the interaction between states and RIOs as well as the role of institutional design features. In doing so, the book sheds light on challenges RIOs are facing in addition to state and organizational features that, when reformed, allow to reduce internal contestations and retain or possibly increase the legitimacy and effectiveness of RIOs as outlets for regional governance.

TWO

Regional International Organizations: Member State Dissatisfaction in Community Organizations

This chapter explains why this book empirically focuses on RIOs as a specific type of IOs. Despite RIOs being often characterized as community organizations (Slocum and van Langenhove 2005, Thomas 2017, Spandler 2018, 2019), member state dissatisfaction can take place concerning a broad variety of RIO policies and (in)activities of a RIO and can give rise to exit threats. While a systematic overview of the grievances of the more than 190 member states of more than 70 RIOs over a longer time frame (1945–2022) is beyond the scope of this book, the section entitled 'Dissatisfaction in RIOs' draws on secondary literature and a media analysis to illustrate with narrative evidence that member states' dissatisfaction vis-à-vis RIOs is widespread – both across states, that is large and small, old and new members, and organizations, including from all regions, old and new RIOs, larger and smaller ones. In other words, it is likely that each member state at one point in time will experience an episode of dissatisfaction with a specific RIO, thereby fulfilling the necessary, yet not sufficient, condition for an exit threat to occur (see Chapter Four for theorizing the latter).

Types of international organizations and rationale for focusing on RIOs

International organizations (IOs) are institutionalized settings, in which three or more states cooperate on the basis of a formal founding treaty, which also specifies the policy areas covered. IOs typically have headquarter offices and a secretariat to support the process of cooperation among the member states. There are different types of IOs (Acharya and Johnston 2007, Panke et al 2020), including: rule-setting/standard-setting versus activity-centered/operational IOs (Vinokurov and Libman 2017, Rittberger et al 2019), democratic versus autocratic IOs (Pevehouse 2005, Debre 2021), China-led versus US-led IOs (Stephen 2021, Heinkelmann-Wild et al 2024a), or global and regional IOs (Acharya and Johnston 2007, Börzel et al 2012a, Söderbaum 2016, Panke et al 2020). Due to the high number of different IO types, most IO studies are selective in terms of which type they focus on, for instance on development IOs only, such as by Pratt (2023).

This book focuses empirically on regional IOs or RIOs. RIOs recruit their membership on the basis of geography-related criteria, while in global IOs all sovereign states can potentially join. Hence, the membership is more limited for RIOs as only those states can potentially become members that are located in a particular regional space. Due to their geography-related membership criteria, RIOs tend to be smaller in size, whereas global IOs usually have a higher number of member states. Moreover, RIO member states tend to be in geographical proximity and therefore often share historical experiences as well as socio-economic and cultural similarities, which frequently go hand-in-hand with high levels of cross-border interactions. Also, due to proximity, RIO member states often face similar contextual or environmental challenges concerning climate or natural disasters, while having opportunities to tackle cross-border problems and interdependencies collectively.

The latter is particularly the case since RIOs are general purpose organizations with broad scopes of policy competencies (Lenz et al 2015, Hooghe and Marks 2015, Panke et al 2020), while global IOs are typically task-specific in nature (Hooghe and Marks 2015, Lenz et al 2015). Yet, unlike most global IOs (the United Nations and especially the United Nations General Assembly being an exception), RIOs tend to be not task-specific but general purpose in the sense that they cover a wide range of issue areas and policy competencies (Lenz et al 2015, Panke et al 2020). Initially, RIOs mainly had competencies in the realms of security and trade, and some, such as NATO, continue to have mandates limited to these areas. However, many other organizations over time have come to include additional policy fields. As a result, RIOs are important outlets for regional governance in areas ranging from economy and trade, security, migration, health, environment, agriculture, and fisheries to human rights and good governance, to name but the most prominent fields (Nolte and Wehner 2013, Haas 2016, Kacowicz and Press-Barnathan 2016, Kim et al 2016, Engel and Mattheis 2019, Lavenex 2019). In addition, over time, RIOs increased in membership size. While in 1960, RIOs had 7.7 member states on average, in 2015, this number had increased to about 13 member states (Panke et al 2020). As RIOs are active in many different policy areas, focusing on a broad variety of substantive issues, most global IOs have highly selective mandates and are active only in a limited number of policy areas, such as telecommunication (International Telecommunications Union), trade (World Trade Organization), or even more narrow issues such as trade in coffee (International Coffee Organization). As a result, the average policy output of global IOs tends to be lower than that of RIOs (Panke et al 2022).

RIOs are also distinct from global IOs as they tend to have higher levels of institutional authority in terms of the pooling of decision-making competencies among member states and their delegation to supranational secretariats (Hooghe et al 2019b). While there are considerable differences among RIOs, decision-making by majority voting, secretariats with substantial competencies, and legalization through the presence of courts are generally more common in RIOs than in the average global IO – excluding exceptional cases such as the World Trade Organization or the International Monetary Fund (Hooghe et al 2017). The greater institutional authority of RIOs is also evident in the fact that many of them have substantial competencies to sanction their member states, for instance by suspending their membership and often make active use of these measures (von Borzyskowski and Vabulas 2019a, Grundsfeld 2024). A rather drastic example is the ECOWAS, which even has the legal authority to militarily intervene in member states without receiving their consent (Hartmann and Striebinger 2015).

While some RIOs have diverse memberships concerning human rights records and regime types, such as the Council of Europe (CoE) or the OAS, others are more homogenous, such as ANDEAN or the GCC. Compared to global IOs, RIOs are more homogenous in nature and member states often share a regional identity so that RIOs can be considered as 'community organizations' (Slocum and van Langenhove 2005, Thomas 2017, Spandler 2019). For example, as one official noted with regards to Southern African Development Community (SADC), while there are differences among the organization's member states, they are 'all Southern Africans, that's something you see if you come from the same part of the world, it's like there's this unity amongst you, whether you know each other or not' (Interview #125, 14/02/2025). Since they are community organizations, exit threats are not made lightly in RIOs. In fact, due to the very nature of being community organizations, RIOs are expected to be least likely cases for member states to express dissatisfaction in the form of exit threats compared to the other IO types. Hence, while discontent should occur among member states of both global and regional IOs as well as other IO types, in this book we focus on RIOs as a least likely but especially relevant type of IO to analyze member states expressing dissatisfaction with organizations through exit threats.

Dissatisfaction in RIOs

We define dissatisfaction as the situation in which member states perceive the organization's policy output (or the absence of a specific policy, politics or polity change) or the RIOs' (in)activities as diverging from their preferences.[1] It is, however, not possible to provide a systematic and encompassing overview of instances of discontent or even the level of (dis)satisfaction for all member states of the more than 70 RIOs over the course of several decades. This is due to two reasons. First, it is difficult to operationalize dissatisfaction. All member states of all RIOs are probably at all points in time *somewhat* displeased with their RIO – in the end, you cannot always get what you want. Second, the fundamental problem concerns the systematic and encompassing identification of instances of disappointment. As discontent can be related to all kinds of substantive issues and be expressed in different ways, it is difficult to capture through a media analysis or the analysis of member state and RIO official reports or homepages based on specific buzzwords, which inevitably entails the risk of a significant number of 'unknown unknowns'. However, the more in-depth qualitative engagement required to identify instances of dissatisfaction for specific member states of RIOs over longer periods of time is not feasible for the large number of cases. As a result, in the following we draw on secondary literature and a cursory media analysis to provide examples of instances of displeasure of member states with their RIOs. Given these inherent limitations, the goal is not to provide a systematic and comprehensive overview over member state grievances in RIOs. Instead, we show that (1) discontent of member states with RIOs is not an exception but (2) affects all kinds of different states and RIOs, so that it is likely that every member state is dissatisfied with a particular RIO at some point, fulfilling the necessary, but not sufficient, condition for an exit threat to occur (see Chapter Four for theorizing the latter).

One example of a state being dissatisfied with a RIO's decision can be found in the Council of Europe. The CoE, established in 1949, is one of the oldest and, with over 45 member states, most comprehensive RIOs in Europe (Panke et al 2020). Besides the Council of Ministers and the Parliamentary Assembly (PACE), the CoE also features the European Court of Human Rights (ECHR), making it one of the RIOs with the most far-reaching competencies in the area of human rights protection (Hooghe et al 2019b). In 2014, the voting rights of the Russian delegation in PACE were suspended following 'the violation of the territorial integrity and sovereignty of Ukraine by the armed forces of the Russian Federation', referring to the annexation of Crimea and Russia's military engagement in eastern Ukraine (PACE 2014, Drezemczewski and Dzehtsiarou 2018). Although the Russian delegation had technically not been sanctioned after 2015 because it had not presented a delegation to PACE, Russia refused to return to the body if the sanction provisions were not eliminated from its rules of procedure (Interview #15, 27/02/2024, Interview #16, 13/03/2024). Russia was severely dissatisfied with the CoE's reaction and, as a consequence, threatened to withdraw (Arbatov and Kolesnikov 2015).

In addition to its refusal to send a delegation to PACE, Russia had also halted its payments to the organization from 2016 onward, thus putting considerable financial pressure on the CoE (Interview #15, 27/02/2024). Its dissatisfaction escalated further when in October 2018 the Secretary General of the CoE, Thorbjorn Jagland, noted that Russia's continued refusal of monetary contributions could lead to its expulsion from the organization (United News of India 2018). In response, Foreign Minister Sergey Lavrov stated that Russia might withdraw from the organization altogether (Trend Daily News 2018). Many member states and the CoE's Secretary General pressured for the reintegration of the Russian delegation into PACE without insisting on conditionalities related to the issues that had led to the suspension in the first place – most importantly the annexation of Crimea (Drezemczewski 2020; Interview #16, 13/03/2024). As a result, in 2019, PACE – under pressure from the Secretary General and the Committee of Ministers (Interview #16, 13/03/2024) – acquiesced to the conditionalities set by Russia for the return of its delegation while also refraining from insisting on any conditionalities towards Russia related to the initial sanctioning (Drezemczewski 2020). This caused considerable dissatisfaction in Ukraine and among several Central and Eastern European states (Interview #14, 26/02/2024). The Ukrainian delegation viewed the Council's policies as 'tantamount to appeasement' (Intellinews 2019). Similarly, Estonian President Kersti Kaljulaid stated that '[t]he reason for these sanctions was a blatant violation of international law by Russia. Not one of the reasons why Russia's voting rights were suspended in 2014 has changed' (ERR 2019). In effect, Estonia and Ukraine were openly dissatisfied with the decision to readmit the Russian delegation.

Another instance of a state having a grievance with a RIO is Paraguay concerning MERCOSUR. The organization had been founded in 1994 by Argentina, Brazil, Paraguay, and Uruguay as an economic integration project (Meissner 2017). While MERCOSUR had initially pursued neoliberal economic policies, it shifted its orientation with the rise to power of left-leaning governments of its member states in the early 2000s during the so-called 'pink tide' (Caballero Santos 2013). As a result, Argentina, Brazil, and Uruguay planned to integrate Venezuela, an associate member since 2006, into the organization (Herz et al 2017). However, this was prevented by the Paraguayan Senate which – while President Fernando Lugo was oriented toward the political left – was dominated by the right-wing conservative Colorado party (Herz et al 2017; Interview #152, 25/03/2025). Lugo, a Roman-Catholic bishop, had become president in 2008 as the candidate of an alliance of parties seeking to remove the Colorado party from power after it had governed the country for the past 61 years (Szucs 2014). In 2012, following violent clashes between the police and farmers in the context of a planned land reform, the Colorado party opened an impeachment proceeding against Lugo (Ezquerro-Cañete and Fogel 2017). Even though the party technically followed the constitutional provisions for such a proceeding, the whole process unfolded in just two days and concluded with Lugo's impeachment (Szucs 2014, San Martim Portes 2017). Given the haste of proceedings and as Lugo had not been given sufficient time to prepare his defense, MERCOSUR regarded the events as a constitutional coup and suspended Paraguay's membership in the organization (Jatobá and Luciano 2018, Ferreira and Paiva 2022; Interview #131, 25/02/2025). Shortly thereafter, the other MERCOSUR members took advantage of this situation by admitting Venezuela as a member into the organization, as this decision could no longer be blocked by the Paraguayan Senate (Weiffen 2017). Whereas Argentina, Brazil, and Uruguay favored Venezuela's accession due to ideological proximity among their left-wing governments and the Venezuelan government of Hugo Chavez as well as due to their interest in Venezuelan oil, the Colorado-led transitional government of Paraguay continued to oppose the accession of Venezuela (Jatobá and Luciano 2018, Ferreira and Paiva 2022). Denouncing this decision as '"illegal" and "null and void"' (Mercopress 2012), the new Paraguayan government was extremely discontent with MERCOSUR's course.

Other examples of severe dissatisfaction with the organization had manifested itself in the form of exit threats by its founding members Uruguay in 2006 and Brazil in 2019 as both countries were intent on signing trade agreements with the US and China, respectively, but were inhibited by organizational statutes prohibiting such bilateral deals (CE Noticias Financieras 2019, CE Noticias Financieras 2023).

Examples of discontent can also be seen in ASEAN. Founded in 1967 as a regional cooperation initiative in Southeast Asia, it remains characterized by extremely informal modes of cooperation based on strict non-intervention and attempts to avoid confrontation (Nair 2019). In 2021, Myanmar experienced a violent military coup in which the country's military retook power from the democratically elected government after a decade of democratic opening up (CFR 2022). In this context, Malaysia, Indonesia, and Singapore opposed the relative leniency of ASEAN toward these events (Interview #129, 25/02/2025). In effect, the three states took a strong stance against Myanmar's junta, which they refused to recognize as the country's legitimate government. This position placed them in clear opposition to other member states: Thailand, for example, took a more accommodating stance against Myanmar (Asia Times 2021; Interview #129, 25/02/2025). While 'member states including Malaysia, Singapore and Indonesia have pushed for [ASEAN] to take action in response to the takeover, others with more authoritarian governments have been less vocal' (AFP 2021). As a result, these countries experienced significant displeasure with ASEAN's reluctant approach toward Myanmar (Interview #94, 28/01/2025).

In other organizations, dissatisfaction is even more widespread. One example is the OAS, the most comprehensive RIO in the Americas. Created in 1948 as the organization for hemispheric cooperation, throughout its history the OAS has been characterized by divergences between the US and Canada, on the one hand, and Latin American states, on the other (Herz 2011, Stapel 2022). More specifically, many Latin American member states are generally discontent with the dominant position taken by the US as well as its economic and even military influence throughout the hemisphere (Weiffen et al 2013). This general discontent sometimes coalesces at specific points in time, for example when the Biden administration disinvited authoritarian-ruled Cuba, Nicaragua, and Venezuela from the 2021 Summit of the Americas, leading several heads of states to boycott the summit and explicitly criticizing this decision (NACLA 2022; Interview #147, 12/03/2025). Prior to that, both Nicaragua and Venezuela had threatened to withdraw from the organization: in the context of its border dispute with Costa Rica in 2010, Nicaragua had harshly criticized the organization's position on the matter and considered withdrawing (Inside Costa Rica 2010), while Venezuela on numerous occasions threatened to withdraw over the OAS's criticism and corresponding resolutions concerning the country's human rights violations (Interview #138, 13/02/2025, Interview #140, 14/02/2025).

Member states also have grievances in the African Union. Founded in 2002 as the successor of the Organization of African Unity (OAU), the AU has been equipped with considerable competencies in the areas of peace and security in addition to mandates in a broad array of policy fields, including economics and trade, environment, and health (Vines 2013, Panke et al 2020). In the security realm, one of the most important measures was the creation of the Peace and Security Council (PSC) in 2003, which was modelled after the UN Security Council. The PSC comprises member states from all five African subregions on a rotating basis and takes decisions concerning the organization's reaction to challenges to peace, security, and governance, such as armed conflicts and military coups (Desmidt 2019). In line with the saying that in the PSC 'everyone wants to be *at* the table, but nobody wants to be *on* the menu', states are regularly displeased with being put on the PSC's agenda, which represents a 'matter of pride' as states often also hold 'animosities' against the AU in this regard (Interview #39, 03/09/2024). However, if the AU drops a certain issue from its agenda, this also creates dissatisfaction, since it is often perceived as unable to manage a particular situation (Interview #39, 03/09/2024). Additionally, discontent also emerges from diverging interpretations of laws and regulations throughout the African continent and across different subregions (Interview #43, 06/09/2024). For example, in 2015, Burundi was irritated with the AU's insistence that President Pierre Nkurunziza's attempt to run for a third term in offices required a referendum (Interview #43, 06/09/2024). States voicing their discontent with the AU is therefore a regular phenomenon in the organization (Interview #41, 05/09/2024).

These examples illustrate that dissatisfaction with RIOs can be linked to a broad variety of reasons. States can be discontent with RIO outputs in the form of the substance or directionality of policies or activities as well as the absence of RIO activity or policies in a given case, as is evident in discontent with actions or lack thereof by the AU's PSC (Interview #39, 03/09/2024). In this respect, the dissatisfaction of member states with RIO output can relate to questions of value attribution as well as regulative questions – such as Estonia's and Ukraine's discontent with the CoE's lenient course towards Russia – or (re)distributive questions, for example in Margaret Thatcher's disappointment with the EU's budget and financing regulations (Backhouse 2002).[2] Moreover, a member state's dissatisfaction can also be linked to RIO polity features, that is the authority of the RIO and its extent of supranationality. An example of the latter is the widespread critique against supranational power accumulation in the EU, both in the context of the Brexit campaign but also by populist challengers more broadly (Kreuder-Sonnen and Zangl 2024). Unlike policy and activity output, which states can achieve in the day-to-day operation of the RIO, changing polity features usually requires treaty changes or amendments, which is not usually subject to day-to-day policy making in the organization, but rather calls for special meetings, such as intergovernmental conferences or conferences of the parties. Also, states can have grievances concerning the activities of specific RIO member states and the (in)activity of the remaining members of the RIO to counteract or prevent the continuation of the criticized behavior or activity, for instance hostility of one member and lack of solidarity of the others. This was evident in the dissatisfaction of Estonia and Ukraine with the CoE's position towards Russia in 2019 (Drezemczewski 2020).

Given the shared history, culture, and geopolitical challenges and opportunities of their members, RIOs are community organizations, and tend to be more homogenous in nature compared to most global IOs (Söderbaum 1996, Spandler 2019). Yet, as this chapter illustrates, despite being community organizations, it is not the case that all member states are always content with all RIO (in)activities. RIOs, unlike global IOs, typically cover a broader set of policy competencies, which can give rise to a broad set of grievances concerning (in)activities of the organization in question.

THREE

Exit Threats as Severe Contestations

The cursory overview in Chapter Two indicates that dissatisfaction of member states with RIOs is widespread. No state and no RIO is eo ipso immune against encountering or being subject to episodes of discontent, which is a necessary condition for exit threats. As outlined, the nature of grievances prevents mapping and systematically quantifying the disappointment of every member state of all 73 RIOs for an extended period of time. This is, however, possible for discontent that is expressed in the form of exit threats. Threats to withdraw are public statements by state officials indicating the state's intention to terminate its membership in the RIO (see von Borzyskowski and Vabulas 2023). Exit threats differ from notifications of withdrawal, which are matter-of-fact statements of a state's already taken decision, and represent expressions of dissatisfaction with the organization linked to the *possibility* of withdrawing from the organization in the future,[1] thereby harming the organization in question by not only publicly showcasing dissent and disharmony, but also by questioning its value as an outlet for institutionalized cooperation and in the process damaging trust and confidence in the organization (Sampson 2017, Leruth et al 2019, Rosamond 2019, von Borzyskowski and Vabulas 2024b, Panke et al 2024).

The phenomenon of exit threats

In recent years, contestations of the liberal international order (LIO) and the (regional) IOs underpinning it have been extensively debated (see for instance Ikenberry 2018, Hooghe et al 2019a, Eilstrup-Sangiovanni and Hofmann 2020, Adler-Nissen and Zarakol 2021, Börzel and Zürn 2021, Debre and Dijkstra 2021, Lake et al 2021, Söderbaum et al 2021). In this regard, recent contributions analyzed the underlying reasons for the contestation of IOs (Kreuder-Sonnen and Rittberger 2023, Dijkstra and Ghassim 2024, Heinkelmann-Wild et al 2024a, Kreuder-Sonnen and Zangl 2024), the strategies of IOs and their bureaucracies for organizational legitimation (Ecker-Ehrhardt 2018, Lenz and Schmidtke 2023, Lenz and Söderbaum 2023, Schmidtke and Lenz 2023, von Billerbeck 2023) and in dealing with internal contestation (Hirschmann 2020, 2021, Schuette and Dijkstra 2023, Dijkstra et al 2025), as well as the occurrence of different forms of contestation of RIOs through their member states (Kreuder-Sonnen and Zangl 2016, Kruck et al 2022, Daßler et al 2022, Daßler et al 2024). Concerning the latter, there has been a thriving debate focusing on one specific form of contestation of IOs: state withdrawals (Brölmann et al 2018, Shi 2018, von Borzyskowski and Vabulas 2019b, 2022, 2024a, 2025, Choi 2022, Dijkstra and Ghassim 2024).

For the 73 RIOs included in the ROCO dataset (for details see 'Empirical pattern: The prevalence of exit threats in RIOs' below), we identify 56 realized exits in the period between 1945 and 2022 (Panke et al 2025a). Withdrawals of member states can have severe consequences for regional and global IOs, potentially leading to processes of 'differentiated disintegration' (Gänzle 2019, Leruth et al 2019), organizational decline (Panke et al 2024), or even their dissolution (von Borzyskowski and Vabulas 2024b). Absent these negative effects, the relations between an IO and a withdrawing state may also be characterized by conflicts, as illustrated by

Brexit (Jurado et al 2022). However, there is another form of contestation that appears to represent a much more widespread phenomenon compared to that of realized exits: during the same period, states threatened to withdraw their membership from these RIOs 123 times – or more than twice as often as the occurrence of executed withdrawals.[2] However, exit threats have received far less scholarly attention. While von Borzyskowski and Vabulas (2023) form a notable exception, they exploratively analyzed the effectiveness of withdrawal threats in achieving IO internal reforms. Yet, they did not analyze the factors contributing to their materialization in the first place.

This gap is surprising, given that exit threats represent significant challenges for RIOs that warrant specific attention. Hence, for three reasons, this book investigates the prevalence of exit threats: first, (regional) IOs are likely to regard exit threats as a major challenge since they are generally not very open to critique. Recent contributions have shown that many (regional) IOs have a very repressive criticism culture (Christian 2022, 2025). While it has long been argued that the bureaucracies of IOs are often characterized by dysfunctions and pathologies (Barnett and Finnemore 2004), Christian (2022, 2025) demonstrates that many IOs also have very restraint criticism cultures, strongly discouraging staff members from voicing criticism and pointing toward organizational mistakes. This is problematic in so far as the voicing and processing of criticism can reasonably be regarded as the first step toward addressing these mistakes and a necessary condition for organizational learning (Christian 2022, 2025). If IOs already regard constructive criticism by staff members as 'a threat rather than a resource' (Christian 2022), unconstructive criticism in the form of exit threats that are voiced by member states – and thus by actors that are considerably more important for an organization than staff members – should be regarded as an immense problem by IOs. It is, consequently, reasonable to assume that, from RIOs' internal point of view, exit threats represent major problems.

Second, threats to withdraw represent important challenges for the affected organizations as they make actual withdrawals more likely. In fact, one in five withdrawals is preceded by exit threats. This endangers RIOs' resource base, political importance, and eventually even their survival. A prime example was ECOWAS, which in 2025 experienced the withdrawal of its three Sahelian member states – Burkina Faso, Mali, and Niger (Kanté et al 2024). ECOWAS had been founded in 1975 as an economic integration project encompassing the whole of West Africa (Müller 2023). The simultaneous loss of three member states represented a predicament for the organization. Since the three Sahel states' economic power was materially negligible, this problem was not primarily one of lost funding or contributions (Interview #96, 29/01/2025). On the one hand, the withdrawal of three member states posed a considerable challenge to future cooperation and the management of coordination problems, including the transnational movement of peoples and goods and the addressing of joint security challenges (Interview #63, 18/09/2024). On the other hand, it also put into question ECOWAS's self-understanding as being the organization inclusive of all West African states (Interview #64, 18/09/2024).

Even if states do not plan to act upon their exit threats, the danger of these threats starting dynamics that may escalate into actual withdrawals always exists. For example, in 2013, 'Prime Minister David Cameron warned […] that unless the European Union reforms to tackle the problems at its heart, Britain risked drifting towards an exit' (AFP 2013). David Cameron, arguably, was not a proponent of Brexit – as indicated by his immediate resignation after the referendum. However, he repeatedly threatened that the UK could withdraw from the EU in order to achieve concessions, for instance regarding the reduction of UK funding obligations to the EU and the free movement of people (Laffan 2021). This was important for Prime Minister Cameron in order to prevail against the strong anti-EU strands in the Tory party, as well as against the newly emerging UK Independence Party (UKIP). While presumably having started with the impression that exit threats would be a controllable risk, they eventually set in motion events that Cameron was ultimately unable to control (Laffan and Telle 2023). Hence, withdrawal threats have the potential to initiate a precarious situation that may eventually result in actual exits.

Third, even if not realized, exit threats nonetheless represent considerable challenges to RIOs. Expressing dissatisfaction, threats to withdraw signal to the outside world that member states regard the RIO as ineffective or illegitimate. By linking critique and demands to the possibility of discontinuing RIO membership, exit threats put into question the legitimacy and utility of the RIO *as such* – and whether the continued operation of the RIO is relevant at all. In this regard, exit threats resemble the contestation of RIOs' validity, which have negative effects on their effectiveness, legitimacy, and resilience (Deitelhoff and Zimmermann 2019, 2020, Zimmermann et al 2023, Panke et al 2025b). This was evident in President Trump's threat to withdraw from NATO. In August 2018, Trump confirmed at a rally that he had threatened to terminate the US's membership at the NATO summit earlier that year: 'Someone said, "would you leave us if we don't pay our bills?" They hated my answer. I said, "Yeah, I would consider it"' (Atlantic Council 2018). In fact, at the 2018 NATO summit, Trump publicly threatening the US's exit from NATO was regarded as a real possibility (Schuette 2021: 1875). As the alliance's most powerful member state, the US's withdrawal threat presented 'an existential challenge questioning both the demand for NATO and the supply of collective defence by NATO' (Dijkstra et al 2024: 8). 'Had Trump carried out his threat to revoke US guarantees in the event that allied defence spending did not meet his demands, this would in effect have terminated the alliance built on the principle of unconditional solidarity in the face of external threats' (Schuette 2021: 1871). The severity of the challenge posed by Trump's withdrawal threat to NATO is also evident in the efforts that the NATO leadership around Secretary General Jens Stoltenberg undertook to appease and distract President Trump in order to prevent him from publicly reiterating his withdrawal threat or to act upon it (Schuette 2021, Dijkstra et al 2024).

Another example of exit threats challenging a RIO's core functions are the repeated threats by Russia in 2018 and 2019 to terminate its membership in the CoE. After the annexation of Crimea in 2014, PACE suspended the voting rights of the Russian delegation – a measure that was renewed in 2015. From 2016 onward, the Russian delegation to PACE had boycotted the body's sessions to avoid renewed sanctions (Drezemczewski and Dzehtsiarou 2018). As the Russian delegation had thus not been able to vote in the elections of several judges to the ECHR, Russia had already publicly questioned whether it would still feel itself to be bound by ECHR rulings (Interview #13, 08/02/2024). This situation escalated with the upcoming elections of the CoE's new Secretary General in 2019. Russia threatened not to recognize the new officeholder and even to withdraw from the organization altogether if it would not be able to vote in the elections (Interview #14, 26/02/2024; United News of India 2018). Russia's exit threat represented a challenge for the CoE. On the one hand, Russia was one of the organization's main financial contributor and the withholding of its funds had already created severe problems for the organization, leading to the suspension and termination of programs and projects (Interview #13, 08/02/2024). On the other hand, Russia's membership in the CoE ensured that the country fell within the jurisdiction of the ECHR, allowing Russian citizens to appeal to the court – which would be impossible if Russia withdrew from the CoE (Interview #12, 08/02/2024). As a result, the CoE, feeling responsible for the over 140 million Russian citizens, regarded a potential Russian exit as a challenge to its core mission (Interview #16, 13/03/2024).

This underlines how the Russian threat to withdraw from the CoE represented a challenge to the organization's material functioning and its self-understanding. In order to prevent Russia's withdrawal, the CoE refrained from insisting on any conditions related to the Russian annexation of Crimea and even followed Russia's call to adjust PACE's rules of procedure to soften sanction provisions (Interview #15, 27/02/2024, Interview #16, 13/03/2024; Drezemczewski 2020).

PIF also provides an illustration of the severe consequences of exit threats. Initially founded as the South Pacific Forum in 1971, the organization is comprised of all small island states in the Pacific along with Australia, New Zealand, and Papua New Guinea (Tarte 2014). In 2020 and 2021, the organization faced exit threats by five of its member states from the Micronesian subregion. The Micronesian PIF member states – Federated States of Micronesia, Kiribati, Marshall Islands, Nauru, and Palau – had expected that the organization's next Secretary General would be from their subregion (The Strait Times 2020). They referred to a reputed 'gentlemen's agreement' dating back to 1978, which foresaw that representatives from the three subregions – Polynesia, Micronesia, and Melanesia – would alternate in holding the position of PIF Secretary General (Fry 2021). In 2021, a candidate from Polynesia was elected for the position and, in response, the five Micronesian states announced their intent to leave the organization (The Japan Times 2022). The threat of countries of one entire subregion to withdraw from the RIO represented a significant challenge to the prospect for future regional cooperation as well as to PIF's self-understanding as the organization representing the entire 'blue pacific continent' (PIF 2022).

Finally, when in 2013 Zimbabwean President Robert Mugabe threatened to withdraw from SADC, this also represented a significant challenge for the organization. The predecessor of SADC, the Southern African Development Co-ordination Conference (SADCC), had been founded in 1980 as an alliance of frontline states to bring an end to the dependence on white minority regimes in the region and contribute to the liberation struggles (Interview #119, 11/02/2025). In the run-up to the 2013 elections in Zimbabwe, SADC, concerned about the elections' democratic credibility, recommended their postponement to implement electoral reforms (Deutsche Welle 2013). In this context, Mugabe's main competitor approached Zimbabwe's constitutional court to seek the election's postponement. In response, Mugabe, during a speech at a rally, threatened to withdraw Zimbabwe from SADC: 'Let it be known that we are in SADC voluntarily; if SADC decides to do stupid things we can move out. No outsider is allowed to intervene in a situation where our courts have made a ruling' (Mail & Guardian 2013). While Zimbabwe's economic power in SADC is relatively limited, its exit threat touched upon the very core of the organization's self-understanding (Interview #115, 10/02/2025). While SADC regards itself as being concerned with safeguarding democratic procedures and values in its member states, its emergence as a coalition of frontline states opposed to white minority rule in Southern Africa represented a crucial aspect of the organization's identity (Interview #118, 11/02/2025, Interview #121, 12/02/2025; Taylor 2016). In effect, the governments that had emerged from former liberation movements are often regarded as a '"club of brother presidents" leading "sister movements"' (Ndlovu-Gatsheni 2011; Interview #126, 14/02/2025). To this end, Robert Mugabe enjoyed considerable standing as an iconic figure of the regional liberation struggles (Interview #127, 16/02/2025, Interview #151, 24/03/2025). As a result, his threat to withdraw from SADC represented a severe challenge to the organization and its internal coherence (Interview #31, 06/08/2024, Interview #126, 14/02/2025).

In effect, exit threats often represent severe challenges for the operation and future functioning RIOs and are, therefore, politically important phenomena. Unlike contestations of RIOs through their member states that merely criticize the organizations, exit threats carry more severe consequences.

Empirical pattern: the prevalence of exit threats in RIOs

Based on a systematic analysis of 73 RIOs for the period between 1945 and 2022, we identify 123 instances of exit threats towards RIOs.[3] For three reasons, we base our analysis of exit threats in regional IOs on the ROCO dataset instead of COW-IGO.[4] First, when comparing the coverage of RIOs between COW-IGO and ROCO, several omissions in the former become apparent, as the ROCO dataset features 18 additional RIOs located across the world, including organizations such as the Asia Cooperation Dialogue (ACD), the Community of Latin American and Caribbean States (CELAC), or the Eastern African Community (EAC), over a time span of 77 years (1945–2022). The ROCO dataset therefore provides a complete sample for the regional IOs subtype, whereas the COW-IGO dataset does not allow for the consideration of a complete sample – neither of global IOs nor regional IOs. Second, the COW-IGO dataset is constrained by instances of missing data as well as coding decisions relating to integration and termination of organizations (Dijkstra and Debre 2022). Finally, the differences between regional and global IOs described in Chapter Two warrant studying both in isolation, whereas a mixed sample risks blurring differences and being unable to make conclusive findings for either type of IO. Overall, the ROCO dataset allows for a more conclusive consideration of our argument.

As outlined above, a notification of withdrawal is a matter-of-fact statement of a state's already taken decision,[5] whereas a withdrawal threat is an expression of dissatisfaction with the RIO linked to the possibility to exit the organization in the future.[6] Therefore, threats to withdraw are not formally included in RIO annual reports or other official accounts. Hence, information on exit threats can only be systematically collected based on a systematic analysis of media sources. We therefore draw on the LexisNexis newspaper database (see also von Borzyskowski and Vabulas 2023). For each RIO and each year of its existence until 2022, we searched for the RIO name and its acronym together with the keywords 'withdr*' and 'exit' respectively to identify the body of relevant newspaper reports. This process was carried out in English, French, Spanish, and Russian, thereby covering the majority of official languages as designated by the RIOs as well as the common languages across their member states.[7] All newspapers within the LexisNexis database were included in the search process. We proceeded in the same way as von Borzyskowski and Vabulas (2023: 5), but go beyond in (1) using two different search terms (also 'exit' and not just 'withdr*'), (2) dropping their search term 'threat*' as the word 'threat' does not have to be stated in order to voice one, and (3) also conducting the search in languages other than English. The identified newspaper articles were subsequently hand-coded in order to establish whether a member state made an exit threat or not.

In terms of the extent to which the respective RIOs are covered by articles within the database, the vast majority indeed has been reported since the establishment or the early years of those organizations (see Table A.2 in the Appendix). While this undoubtedly strengthens the representativeness claim, underrepresentation in the overall picture of generated exit threats can still occur. For instance, some threats to withdraw from an organization might not be voiced explicitly in public by a member state but articulated implicitly behind closed doors (Lipscy 2015, 2017). Such a potential 'tip of the iceberg' scenario has previously been faced within other strands of scholarship, for example compliance research (Börzel et al 2012b), whereby a definitive judgement of the comprehensiveness of the data utilized was impossible. Similarly, it cannot be conclusively ruled out that additional exit threats might have gone unrecorded prior to the first recorded withdrawal in 1967. Yet, all efforts were made to ensure that the universe of exit threats is exhaustive.

All results were subsequently hand-coded to further ascertain whether an exit threat had in fact been made or not. As our unit of analysis is state-IO-year (see Chapter Four), a maximum of one threat per member state per RIO per year was recorded, even if the state in question might have reiterated an exit threat several times in a given year. During the coding process, cases were excluded primarily for three reasons. First, no exit threat was coded when newspapers reported on statements by opposition politicians or politicians not in an executive function in the government. According to our definition, exit threats must be stated by the state's government, that is, people in executive positions or the institutions that they represent.[8] Second, we also excluded instances in which a state only threatened to terminate its participation in or support for a specific RIO body as opposed to the organization as such.[9] Finally, we did not code as exit threats newspapers reports on actual realized exits or mere notifications of exit that are not linked to a threat.[10] Whereas notifications of exits simply inform the organization of a member's already finalized decision to withdraw and do not leave room for compromise to reverse the decision, threats to withdraw allow for concessions and can be taken back or not acted upon should the position of the state be accommodated by the RIO so that the grounds for dissatisfaction and the exit threat no longer persist.

Empirically, exit threats vary between states and organizations. From 1945 to 2022, there were 123 instances of threats to withdraw from RIOs issued by a total of 65 different countries (see Figure 3.1). Morocco and Russia, respectively, voiced their grievances through threats to walk out in six instances, while Belarus articulated five threats and the UK and Kazakhstan both made four threats. 29 countries each threatened once to exit a RIO, such as Argentina in the OAS in 1980, Armenia in the OSCE in 2006, Cameroon in the AU in 1980, or Papua New Guinea in the Pacific Community (SPC) in 1982.

A total of 27 RIOs in the Americas, Africa, and Europe were subject to exit threats (see Figure 3.2). The most threats were articulated in the AU (14), followed by PIF (13), the Eurasian Economic Union (EAEU) (9), the Organisation

EXIT THREATS AS SEVERE CONTESTATIONS

Figure 3.1: Exit threats by country (1945–2022)

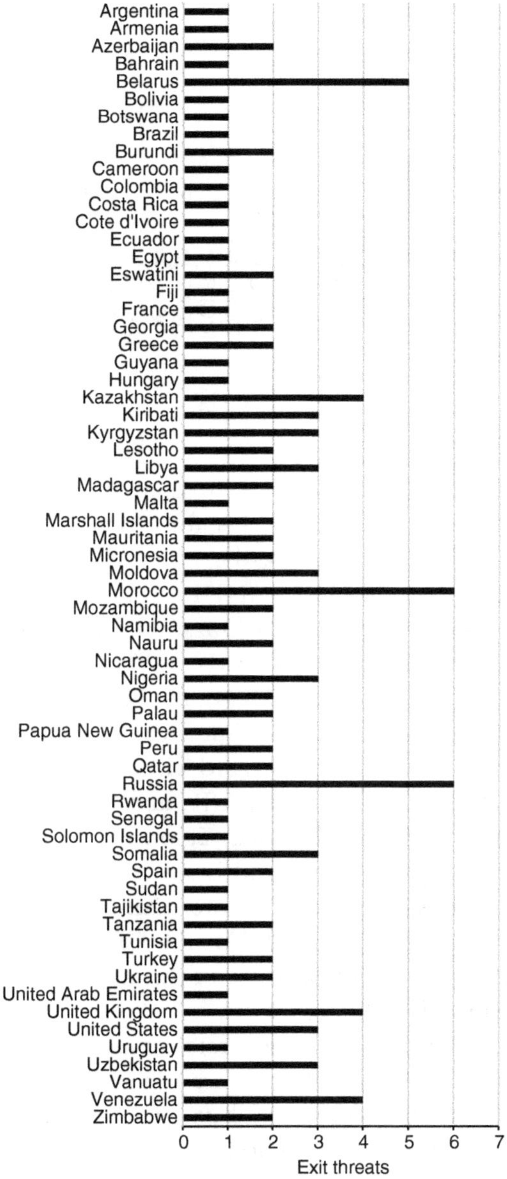

Figure 3.2: Exit threats experienced by RIO (1945–2022)

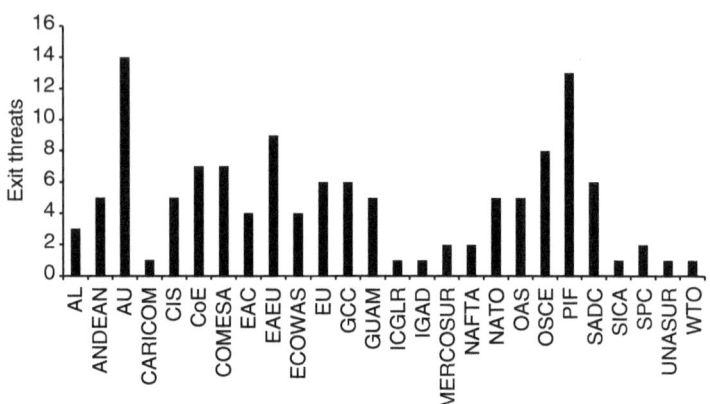

for Security and Co-operation in Europe (OSCE) (8), the CoE, and the Common Market for Eastern and Southern Africa (COMESA) (7 each), the EU, GCC, and SADC (6 each), Andean Community (ANDEAN), Commonwealth of Independent States (CIS), Organization for Democracy and Economic Development (GUAM), NATO, and the OAS (5 each), the EAC and ECOWAS (4), the League of Arab States (LAS) (3), Mercado Comun del Sur (MERCOSUR), NAFTA and SPC (2), as well as one threat to withdraw in CARICOM, ICGLR, IGAD, SICA, UNASUR, and the Warsaw Treaty Organization (WTO). In Asia, regionalism took off much later than in other regions and is still evolving (Panke et al 2020), which is reflected in a lower number of RIOs being located in Asia and fewer RIO memberships of states in this region, as well as by the absence of threats to withdraw from these organizations.

Finally, there is only a moderate temporal trend towards an increasing number of exit threats in general. Especially during the last decade, threats have increased, with the year 2022 constituting an exception by featuring a lower-than-average number (see Figure 3.3). This trend corresponds

EXIT THREATS AS SEVERE CONTESTATIONS

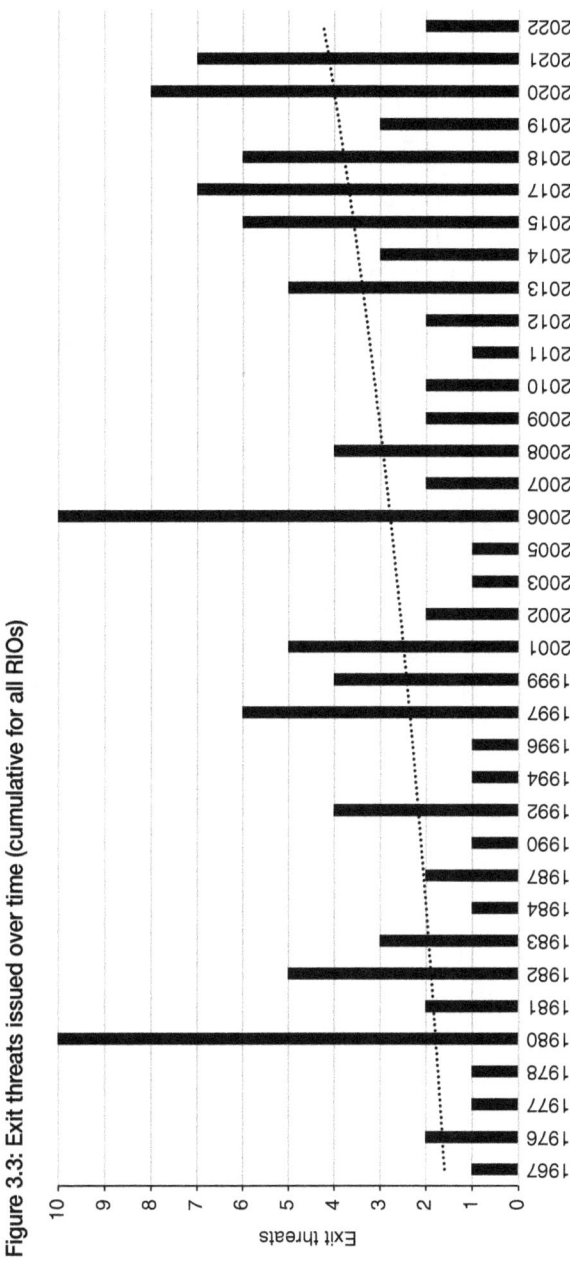

Figure 3.3: Exit threats issued over time (cumulative for all RIOs)

to an increase in the number of RIOs created and the fact that these organizations increase in size over time as newly independent states join existing organizations. Also, several of the RIOs created in the last decades featured more members from their onset.

To complement state of the art insights into severe contestations of (R)IOs and study what influences the chances that states voice their dissatisfaction by threatening to withdraw from an organization, this book addresses the following research question: Why does the prevalence of exit threats differ between and within RIOs? As a first step towards answering this question, the subsequent chapter introduces the theoretical model used and discusses the corresponding hypotheses.

FOUR

A Systems Theory Perspective on the Prevalence of Exit Threats

This chapter provides the theoretical framework to account for the observed variation in the prevalence of exit threats in and between RIOs (see Chapter Three), which is subsequently put to an empirical plausibility probe (Chapter Five).

Dissatisfaction with respect to individual IO policies or IO (in)activities is not a rare phenomenon – as the tip of the iceberg analysis with respect to RIOs suggests (see Chapter Two). Hence, no state and no organization is immune from encountering instances of discontent. Nevertheless, it is not the case that each member state automatically expresses its displeasure with an organization's policy or (in)activity by issuing an exit threat. This suggests that dissatisfaction, while being necessary, is not a sufficient condition for exit threats being voiced.

To explain why the prevalence of exit threats differs between and within organizations, we draw on Easton's systems theory (Easton 1965). Easton's theory provides an abstract model of the functioning and persistence of political systems as 'interactions within a society concerned with the authoritative allocation of values' (Fuhse 2005: 27; see also Figure 4.1). Given its considerable level of abstraction, Easton's model can be applied to various political systems (Rittberger et al 2019), including different types of IOs, such as regional or global IOs, rule-setting/standard-setting or activity-centered/ operational IOs. IOs are also concerned with the – more or less – authoritative allocation of values for a group of states

(Easton 1965: 284–5; Fuhse 2005: 30). Although this book empirically studies one specific type of IO, namely RIOs (see 'Types of international organizations and rationale for focusing on RIOs' in Chapter Two for more details), neither the theoretical framework nor the corresponding hypotheses are specific to RIOs. Instead, both are of a general nature and can in principle be applied to all types of IOs.[1] Easton's theoretical framework focuses on the role of specific and diffuse support for the persistence of political systems. States withdrawing their support for organizations represent the starting point of the research on the contestation of IOs (Kreuder-Sonnen and Zangl 2016, Copelovitch and Pevehouse 2019, Hirschmann 2021, Daßler et al 2022, Kruck et al 2022, Kreuder-Sonnen and Rittberger 2023, Dijkstra et al 2024, Heinkelmann-Wild et al 2024a). States' support for IOs is also closely connected to perceptions of organizations' legitimacy. In recent years, a vast literature has analyzed the role of legitimacy for international organizations (Dellmuth and Tallberg 2015, Bäckstrand et al 2018, Bearce and Jolliff Scott 2019, Sommerer et al 2022), along with factors at the societal and individual level (Ecker-Ehrhardt 2012, Dellmuth and Tallberg 2015, Schmidtke 2019, Dellmuth and Tallberg 2020, Dellmuth et al 2022a, Dellmuth et al 2022b, Dellmuth and Tallberg 2023, Houde 2023, Spandler and Söderbaum 2023), as well as those on the IO-level (Badache 2022, Dellmuth et al 2019), that contribute to (individual-level) perceptions of the legitimacy or illegitimacy of IOs (Bernauer et al 2019, Dingwerth et al 2019a). The importance of support for IOs is also evident in the fact that IOs have widely engaged in processes of self-legitimation (Gronau and Schmidtke 2015, Ecker-Ehrhardt 2018, Bexell et al 2020, von Billerbeck 2020, 2023, Lenz and Schmidtke 2023, Lenz and Söderbaum 2023, Schmidtke and Lenz 2023). Easton's systems theory provides an avenue to integrate these approaches into an overarching framework that links the occurrence of exit threats in the face of dissatisfaction to the specific and diffuse support that states' hold towards an IO – and allows explaining variation in the occurrence of exit threats between states and IOs.

The central elements of Easton's model are actors' demands toward the political system, the outputs produced by the system, and the feedback loop connecting them (Easton 1965: 26, see Figure 4.1).

Demands as inputs into the political system represent calls for the authoritative allocation of values through output in a specific way (Easton 1965: 38–41). They constitute a given without which no political system could exist (Easton 1965: 37). All states, in one way or another, formulate demands for the authoritative allocation of values as inputs into IOs they are members of. Examples include state demands for the (re)distribution of financial or informational resources among member states, the setting of regulatory standards in a specific policy area or concerning a specific issue, the conduct or orchestration of activities such as peacekeeping operations, or the demand for symbolic legitimacy through the IO – that is by serving as a platform for summits or non-binding symbolic declarations – while not producing specific policy outputs or engaging in certain

Figure 4.1: A systems theory perspective on exit threats

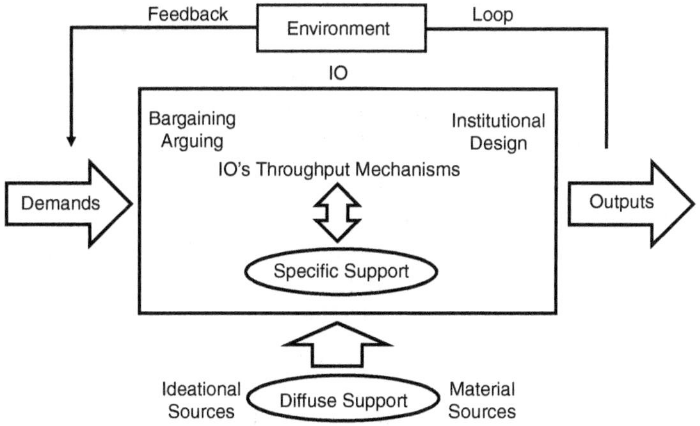

Source: Based on Easton (1965)

activities (Vinokurov and Libman 2017, Vinokurov 2017, Russo and Stoddard 2018). Demands are reflective of states' satisfaction or dissatisfaction with the IO. When states face the situation of being displeased with the organization, this discontent gives rise to demands that states direct towards the IO in order to address their dissatisfaction by IOs' outputs reflecting their demands.

Just as all member states always have demands vis-à-vis IOs, IOs as political systems also always, in one way or another, produce outputs in the form of policies, activities or legitimation of its members (Easton 1965: 343–50). Notwithstanding that some IOs create few tangible outputs based on their respective policy mandates (Stoddard 2017, Vinokurov and Libman 2017, Gray 2018, Libman and Obydenkova 2020, Gast 2023), according to the broad understanding in Easton's model, also immaterial outputs – statements, meetings, or even non-decisions – represent outputs produced by the political system.

IOs' outputs affect their external environment, which consists of states – both members and third party states – other IOs, as well as all kinds of domestic and transnational actors. In effect, the external environment is the entire 'context' in which the IO operates, which it influences through its output, and through which its members are also affected. More specifically, the external environment gives rise again to demands that member states direct toward the IO (Easton 1965: 71–3, 366–71). Even though IO outputs are as broad and indeterminate as the demands directed toward them, what is relevant for the feedback loop between outputs and demands is not the outputs produced or their effects on the external international environment, but their evaluation by the member state (Easton 1965: 382–91). As a result, given that demands, outputs, and the feedback loop connecting them are ubiquitous and idiosyncratic, in this short book we bracket this part and do not specifically theorize them. Instead, we focus on the aspect of states' support for the IO as a political system (Easton 1965: 153–7). More specifically, based on Easton's system theory, we argue that a member state – when encountering a situation of dissatisfaction – becomes increasingly likely to issue an exit threat toward an IO the more limited its specific and its diffuse support for the organization (Easton 1965: 220–5).

Specific support

Specific support depends on states' general ability to influence RIOs' throughput mechanisms and the chance of transforming demands into outputs (Easton 1965: 267–8, 401–3). Though demands, throughput, and outputs represent a continuous cycle, a state is increasingly likely to revert to exit threats when, from its perspective, this sequence is disrupted as it is unable to shape the organization's output according to its own demands. Therefore, specific support is not about a state being able to effectively address its grievances in each case and have its demands translated into the desired IO outputs each and every time. Instead, it is the possibility of a state to influence the throughout process in a way that allows for a good chance that its demands are reflected in the IO's outputs.

Easton's original formulation of the model treats the political system as a black box, thus bracketing the politics, or throughput mechanisms, by which the political system transforms demands into outputs. We argue that states' general chance to exert influence on IOs' throughput mechanism depends on country and institutional design features. Country features refer to a member state's ability to generally influence the decision-making process. Negotiation processes in IOs entail aspects of both bargaining, by which states voice demands linked to costs and benefits to press for concessions, and arguing, by which states voice arguments to persuade others that a specific solution is appropriate for a specific problem (Risse 2000, Müller 2004, Panke 2010c).[2] Empirical research has illustrated that arguing and bargaining usually coexist in negotiations among states (Johnstone 2003, Börzel et al 2010, Risse and Kleine 2010).

When bargaining dynamics are at play, a state's ability to translate demands into outputs in IO decision-making increases the greater the ideological similarity to the fellow member states and the more resources it can draw on, as both aspects bring advantages during bargaining. Well-resourced states are more powerful and better equipped to shape decisions in IOs (Moravcsik 1998). They can exert pressure on fellow member states by threatening retaliatory measures or offering side payments (Kuziemko and Werker 2006, Milewicz and Snidal 2016). Additionally, powerful states are also likely to have a greater influence over IO outputs, as they can threaten to withhold relevant resources – in terms of finance or expertise – from the organization. Accordingly, powerful states' preferences often represent the default condition that IO bureaucracies tend to align with (Clark and Dolan 2020, Pouliot 2017). In addition, when bargaining takes place, a state is – *ceteris paribus* – in a better position to get what it wants the closer its own win-set is to the win-set of the other member states as the concessions to be made to reach a negotiation outcome are less demanding and less encompassing (Putnam 1988). In other words, the greater the ideological similarity of a state to the other member states, the greater the chances that its demands are reflected in the political system's outputs. Conversely, if a state is ideologically far apart from fellow member states, it is generally less able to exert influence over the IO's outputs.

Further, well-resourced states are also likely to have a greater influence in argumentative processes of decision-making (Panke 2010a, Adler-Nissen and Pouliot 2014, Panke et al 2018). Being able to afford better staffed, trained, and equipped – or in other words, more effective – diplomatic representation in the IO (Panke et al 2021) makes a state more powerful, as it is in a better position to influence IO internal arguments due to superior expertise, preparation, and experience (Börzel et al 2010, Pouliot 2016). Moreover, states' ability to influence decision-making processes in an IO also depends on the presence of conditions conducive to argumentative action. According to a 'logic of arguing', better arguments prevail in the process reaching a reasoned output to which all can agree (Habermas 1995b, Risse 2000, Mitzen 2005, Panke 2010c). While IOs generally represent conducive environments for the exchange of arguments (Milewicz and Goodin 2016), a crucial factor for effective arguing is a shared lifeworld providing the states with a shared yardstick to assess the quality of arguments and establish intersubjective validity instead of talking at cross-purposes (Habermas 1995b, Risse 2000, Börzel et al 2010, Panke 2010a). The closer a state is in ideological terms to the other IO member states, the more it shares a common lifeworld with the others. This increases the general chances for effective arguing by which a state convinces fellow member states of the rightfulness or appropriateness of specific IO outputs.

The ability of an individual state to be in a good position to generally exert influence in the throughput phase of IOs via arguing or bargaining can also be influenced by organizational features, most notably the decision-making rules (Goldstein et al 2000, Hooghe et al 2019b, Hooghe and Marks 2015) and the scope of policy competencies covered (Lenz and Marks 2016, Panke et al 2020). These features might impact the chances of an individual state to make its voice heard in the throughput stage and ensure that its demands are sufficiently echoed in IO outputs. If a state cannot effectively address its grievances in the IO's policy-making process (throughput stage) in the long run, this inability is bound to reduce its specific support for the organization, which increases the chances for exit threats.

Characterized by different extents of pooling of decision-making competencies among member states (Hooghe et al 2019b, Hooghe and Marks 2015), IOs differ in terms of how they organize institutional authority. For example, while the Summit of the Arctic Council or the Conference on Disarmament take decisions by consensus, the General

Assembly and Permanent Council of the OAS decide by two-thirds majorities, and the EU's Council of Ministers operates on qualified majority voting, whereas the International Labour Organization utilizes simple majority. Consensus rule grants each state a veto and allows to prevent IO outputs that do not sufficiently reflect a state's demands, and majority voting reduces the number of states required to be brought on board to pass a decision. As a result, majority rule creates situations in which individual states can be outvoted in the throughput stage and consequently cannot translate their demands into IO outputs (Koremenos et al 2001, Blake and Payton 2015). This reduces the general shaping ability of a member state and thereby the specific support attributed to the organization, which correspondingly increases the chances for exit threats to take place.[3]

Although RIOs tend to be multipurpose organizations (Panke et al 2020) whereas global IOs are primarily task-specific (Lenz et al 2015), the policy scope covered can also differ within global as well as within regional IOs. For instance, the United Nations is a global IO, covering all policy fields, while NATO is a RIO equipped only with competencies in the issue areas of security and also ammunition-related competencies in the issue area of trade.

The policy competencies with which an IO is equipped is defined by its treaties and explicates the number and scope of different substantive issues that member states negotiate in the throughput stage (Panke et al 2025). In general, a broader scope of policy competencies of an IO can increase the chances that a state fails to sufficiently shape all outputs according to its own demands. Correspondingly, reduced specific support should increase the likelihood of exit threats in IOs with broader policy scopes.

Irrespective of whether bargaining or arguing dominates in a specific negotiation, a state that is well-resourced and ideologically similar to the other members should be in a better position to have its demands reflected in the IO's outputs (Panke 2010, Panke 2013), which should also increase if the IO in question is operating on the basis of consensus rule and when the policy scope covered by the organization is limited in nature. Under these conditions, a state is more likely to attribute specific support to the IO in question in the longer term and is, consequently, less likely to voice exit threats when a situation emerges in which the state in question indeed fails to translate its demands into IO outputs and experiences, which amounts to a situation of dissatisfaction. By contrast, ill-resourced states that are ideologically dissimilar to the average IO member state are more likely to fail in translating their demands into IO outputs, which over time reduces specific support and increases the chances that the state in question resorts to exit threats, which is also increasingly likely when the respective organization has majority decision-making and a broad policy scope.

Hypothesis 1 on specific support therefore expects: the likelihood for exit threats increases when states are generally unlikely to turn their demands in an organization's policy-making process into desired outputs due to state features (limited power, ideological dissimilarity) and organizational features (majority rule, broad policy scope).

Diffuse support

While specific support towards IOs results from states' general ability to influence the transformation of demands into outputs in the organization, diffuse support refers to normative attitudes towards the IO as a political system (Easton 1965: 273–4). This includes a sense of 'we-ness' and community feeling that actors direct toward the political system, as well as the trust they put into and the legitimacy they attribute to it (Easton 1965: 278–82, 289–90; Fuhse 2005: 42–3). It is for this reason connected to support due to a logic of appropriateness (March and Olsen 1998).

Easton argues that diffuse support for a political system depends on actors' socialization (Easton 1965: 306–10; Fuhse 2005: 44). States' diffuse support for an IO should increase the more they are socialized into the organization. The starting point for arguments about socialization in IOs is to regard them as social environments (Barnett and Finnemore 2004, Adler-Nissen 2014, Pouliot 2016). Identification with an organization may initially be low but is likely to increase over time as an effect of member states' socialization into it. Socialization thereby takes the form of social learning processes through participation in the organization's practices, which leads to the adoption of common taken-for-granted assumptions, dispositions, and understandings as well as loyalty with and generalized support for the political systems (Adler 2019). These processes are supported by dynamics of social pressure, as members of the organization reward conforming and punish non-conforming behaviors (Johnston 2001). Several studies provided evidence in favor of the socializing effects of IO membership on states (Checkel 2004, Kelley 2004, Murdoch et al 2018), for instance in the form of convergence in terms of interests (Bearce and Bondanella 2007) and human rights practices (Greenhill 2010; Risse et al 2013). In any case, the decisive point is that socialization is a long-term process (Fuhse 2005: 43–4): in the context of organizations, it takes place through social learning and pressure while unfolding over longer periods, thereby increasing member states' diffuse support toward the organization. In this respect, the duration of a state's membership in an IO is relevant for the extent of its socialization within the organization and identification with it, which, in turn, generates diffuse support and reduces the likelihood of exit threats when a situation emerges in which a state experiences dissatisfaction with a specific RIO output or RIO (in)activity. In other words, diffuse support buffers situations in which a state fails effectively to address its grievances as it cannot translate its demand into the desired IO output. While states should be more socialized into the IO the longer they have been a member, an IO that exists over a long period of time should attract more diffuse support than a recently created IO. When comparing IOs, we would therefore expect that established ones receive – *ceteris paribus* – fewer exit threats than those more recently created.

Another source of diffuse support for IOs relates to the level of democracy. Research on the democratic peace argues that governments of democratic states externalize their domestic orientation toward compromise and non-violent decision-making rules (Risse-Kappen 1995, Gartzke 1998). As a result, democratic states display, on average, greater support for institutionalized multilateral cooperation and are more active in the creation of IOs (Panke 2020). Building on this insight, subsequent research has extensively analyzed connections between characteristics of domestic political regimes and public perceptions of IO legitimacy. In this regard, Agné et al (2015) argue that societal actors' perception of IOs' legitimacy depends on the level of domestic democracy. Additionally, recent research on public perceptions of IOs found strong connections between domestic institutional trust and trust in IOs (Dellmuth and Tallberg 2020, Dellmuth et al 2022a, Dellmuth et al 2022b). Dellmuth and Tallberg (2015) find that the most important factor explaining public perceptions of IO legitimacy is trust in domestic political institutions as well as citizens' support for democracy as a system of governance – both of which tend to be greater in democratic states (Ecker-Ehrhardt et al 2024). Further, Dellmuth and Tallberg outline that beliefs in the legitimacy of both domestic and international institutions are caused by the antecedent factor of generalized social trust, which is most significant in established democracies (2020: 316). Similarly, IOs are increasingly emphasizing the democratic value of their procedures as legitimating strategies (Dingwerth et al 2019a, Schmidtke and Lenz 2023). As a result, governments of democratic member states should be more accustomed to principles such as rule-based governance, legitimate dissent, the validity of compromises, as well as the acceptance of varying majority–minority patterns and the situation of being on the winning side for one decision and the losing side for another, while regarding IOs as generally more legitimate. Hence, democratic states should attribute greater generalized support to the IO in question compared to more authoritarian members and are therefore less likely to express individual grievances by resorting to exit threats. Likewise, the overall level of democracy in an IO impacts political practices and interactions between the member states as it defines which behavior is regarded as appropriate in line with democratic principles (Tallberg et al 2016). When democratic norms are prevalent in IOs, this might reduce contestation practices and stop them from escalating as states follow a script of appropriateness, according to which it is normatively expected from one another to accept IO decisions and negotiated compromises, even when being dissatisfied with the particularities (Dellmuth and Tallberg 2014).

Accordingly, *hypothesis 2* on diffuse support states: the likelihood for exit threats increases when the commitment to an IO is limited, due to state features (short membership duration, autocracy) and organizational features (limited IO age, autocratic IO).

Table 4.1 (see opposite page) summarizes the hypotheses derived from Easton's systems theory.[4] They are complementary in nature and not mutually exclusive, thereby reflecting the multicausal dynamics at play in political systems.

Applying Easton's theory to different types of IOs

Empirically, this book studies one specific type of IOs, namely RIOs (see Chapter Two). Yet, neither the theoretical framework nor the corresponding hypotheses are specific to RIOs. Instead, theory and hypotheses are of a general nature and can be applied to all types of IOs: rule-setting/standard-setting versus activity-centred/operational IOs (Vinokurov

Table 4.1: Overview of hypotheses

Hypotheses	
H1: *Specific support*	The likelihood for exit threats increases when states are generally unlikely to turn their demands in an organization's policy-making process into desired outputs, due to state features (limited power, ideological dissimilarity) and organizational features (majority rule, broad policy scope).
H2: *Diffuse support*	The likelihood for exit threats increases when the commitment to an IO is limited, due to state features (short membership duration, autocracy) and organizational features (limited IO age, autocratic IO).

and Libman 2017, Rittberger et al 2019), democratic versus autocratic IOs (Pevehouse 2005, Debre 2021), China-led versus US-led IOs (Stephen 2021, Heinkelmann-Wild et al 2024a) or regional and global IOs (Acharya and Johnston 2007, Börzel et al 2012a, Söderbaum 2016, Panke et al 2020).

The hypotheses on specific and diffuse support relate to member state and organizational level features and explain variation in the prevalence of exit threats within and between IOs. Yet, depending on which type of IO one studies empirically, the theory suggests differences in the prevalence of exit threats – either linked to features of member states or organizational features.

Comparing democratic with autocratic IOs (Pevehouse 2005, Debre 2021, Debre 2025), we would expect differences concerning diffuse support. Under *ceteris paribus* conditions, democratic norms of rule-based governance, legitimate dissent, the validity of compromises, as well as the acceptance of varying majority–minority patterns increase diffuse support not only among democratic member states but also in democratic IOs. This is expected to reduce the prevalence of exit threats in democratic compared to autocratic IOs. A similar expectation would be in order for the distinction between US-led and China-led IOs – at least before the populist government took office in the US.

When zooming into rule-setting/standard-setting versus activity-centered/operational IOs (Vinokurov and Libman 2017, Rittberger et al 2019), we would expect specific support to be higher in the latter than the former, but only under a specific condition: rule-setting and standard-setting IOs can be of general purpose character or cover only a specific policy field. By contrast, activity-centered or operational organizations are always task-specific, such as the International Atomic Energy Agency, which is tasked with furthering the peaceful use of nuclear technology and nuclear power, thereby lowering the chances for exit threats somewhat compared to the average rule-setting and standard-setting IOs.

Comparing RIOs with global IOs (see also Chapters One and Two), organizational and country-level factors are likely to vary empirically. In line with the notion that RIOs are community organizations, the ideological divergence among member states should be lower in the average RIO compared to the average global IO, as the global IO has more member states that are recruited from across the globe (Pevehouse et al 2020). Accordingly, the heterogeneity between member states is most likely higher than in RIOs, in which a lower number of states share socio-economic and historical ties and experiences and often face the same environmental or contextual challenges and opportunities (Panke et al 2020). Thus, differences in membership composition are likely to be empirically reflected in differences concerning ideological divergence in IOs, which should reduce the prevalence of exit threats in RIOs compared to global IOs. Similarly, global IOs, due to being larger in membership size, often feature greater power disparities among their member states compared to RIOs (Panke et al 2018). This goes hand in hand with a higher share of weak member states that are, other factors being equal, in a disadvantageous position to translate their demands into outputs as part of IO decision-making. Compared to a global IO, exit threats should be less prevalent in RIOs. Also, specific support, based on the ability of a member state to address its demands in the policy process so that they are reflected by IO outputs, should be somewhat higher in global IOs compared to RIOs, as the latter more often operate on the basis of majority decision-making, when being outvoted is possible (Hooghe et al 2017, Hooghe et al 2019b). In contrast, we would expect that global IOs attract fewer exit threats due to narrower scopes of policy competencies in light of their task-specific nature (Hooghe et al 2017); whereas the typical RIO is general purpose in nature and has often competencies in economy and trade, security and defense, environment, agriculture and fisheries, health development or infrastructure domains (Panke et al 2020). Although the theory can be applied to all types of IOs (global and regional IOs, rule-setting/standard-setting and activity-centered/operational IOs, democratic and autocratic IOs, or China-led and US-led IOs), when considering the differences between global and regional IOs, we expect – on average – exit threats to be less prevalent in regional compared to global IOs.

FIVE

Empirical Analysis: Accounting for the Varying Prevalence of Exit Threats

This chapter initially discusses methodological choices with respect to the data sample and the measurement of exit threats as well as the operationalization of the explanatory variables. Subsequently, it puts the expectations derived from Easton's systems theory to an empirical test by combining regression analysis with qualitative narrative evidence before discussing the findings.

Operationalization and methodology

This book empirically studies exit threats of states that are members of RIOs. While the theoretical argument put forward is not restricted to a particular type of IO as the hypotheses developed in Chapter Four do not depend on particular features or conditions inherent to specific IOs, and are broadly applicable, we test the argument in the subsample of regional IOs, namely the extended ROCO 2.0 dataset (Panke et al 2020; see Chapter Three). The empirical analysis includes 73 RIOs between 1945 and 2022. The *dependent variable* is whether or not a state issues a threat to withdraw from a given organization in a given year (see Chapter Three) and the unit of analysis is accordingly the state-RIO-year. When a state is a member of an organization in a particular year, this is coded with '0' and with '1' if an exit threat is voiced in a given RIO and year.

If a state is not, or no longer, a member of a RIO, this is coded as a missing value (.).

The *independent variables* are operationalized in the following manner (summary statistics are provided in Table A.3). Hypothesis 1 focuses on specific support. It relates to the throughput component of Easton's systems theory and captures the chances that a state's demands or inputs can generally be turned into RIO outputs (see also Table 4.1). The chances for generalized individual influence of a member state depend on both country and organizational features. For country features, we include measures on ideational (dis)similarity as well as the relative power of a state in a RIO. RIOs are general purpose organizations and do not focus on a single task or issue. Accordingly, we capture potential ideational divergence of member states not by security, environment, or economic indicators, but through general differences among member states based on their regime type. To this end, we calculated the absolute divergence of a member state from the RIO mean of the imputed Polity IV and Freedom House data per year (see Dahlberg et al 2022). While state power in RIOs can be captured by proxies based on a country's size or its economic performance, most studies use the latter (Keohane 1989, Barnett and Duvall 2004, Zartman and Rubin 2009, Gómez-Mera 2013). Accordingly, we also opt for a GDP-based measure and use time-series data on GDP in current USD stemming from the World Bank. As power is an inherently relational concept, we use a relative economic power measure, calculated by subtracting the RIO mean in a given year from the country's power in a given year.

For the organizational features of hypothesis 1, we focus on the policy scope of the IO as well as a majority rule (pooling). The scope of a RIO's policy mandate is measured by the number of different policy competencies an organization is equipped with at a given point in time. The data stems from the ROCO 2.0 dataset and captures a total of 344 different policy competencies (see Panke et al 2020). The possibility of an individual state being overruled in IO decision-making is captured by majority rule. The variable is coded with '1' if majority decisions are possible in a RIO in a given year, and with '0' otherwise. The data for this variable stems from the ROCO dataset (see Panke et al 2020).

Hypothesis 2 focuses on the role of diffuse support, capturing general normative attitudes towards the organization in question (see Table 4.1). We expect that democracies place greater value on cooperation in general and are socialized into political systems in which today's losers can become tomorrow's winners. Accordingly, such states attribute greater diffuse support to the RIO and have a higher tolerance for encountering a situation in which they failed to exert influence in line with their demands at a given point in time. Vice versa, autocracies are not as strongly socialized into cooperation and are expected to be more prone to respond to instances of dissatisfaction with an organization by voicing exit threats. The extent to which a country is democratic is measured by imputed data from Freedom House and Polity IV datasets and ranges between '0' (lowest) to '10' (highest) (see Dahlberg et al 2022). Based on the same data, we calculate the RIO mean, which captures whether an organization tends to be autocratic or democratic in nature. The hypothesis expects that autocratic IOs are subject to more exit threats, whereas a democratic culture in the IO should buffer against instances of member state dissatisfaction from turning into an exit threat.

Moreover, membership duration is also expected to influence diffuse support. The longer a state has been a member of a specific organization, the more likely it became socialized into the respective IO, which creates loyalty and feeds into diffuse support. This form of diffuse support is measured by the number of years a state has been member in a given IO (data stems from the ROCO dataset). Finally, IOs have more chances to socialize their members by creating and strengthening normative commitment the older the organization in question is. To capture the age of the IO in question, we calculated the number of years since the creation of the organization (information stems from ROCO dataset).

Furthermore, we control for IO size, the presence or absence of a withdrawal clause in the IO's legal texts, the presence of absence of courts (delegation), the possibility of a contagion effect, interstate conflicts between IO members, the presence of a regional hegemon, and the extent of regime complexity. The summary statistics are provided in the Appendix (Table A.3).

As regional IOs tend to be more selective in terms of member states than global IOs, based on the geography-related membership criterion (see above), we control for the size of the organization. RIO size is measured by the number of member states in a given organization and year. This information stems from the ROCO dataset and has been extended based on RIO homepages to cover the years up till 2022 (see Panke et al 2020).

The negotiation literature claims that bargaining chips are most effective when the threat is credible (Druckman 1977, Plantey 2007, Slapin 2008). In this sense, exit threats might be more prevalent when RIO treaties explicate the process of withdrawals. At the same time, however, states can use such threats as a means to extract concessions from fellow members (von Borzyskowski and Vabulas 2023, see also 'From talking the talk to walking the walk'). This presupposes that exit threats can be taken back or not acted upon once a concession has been granted, which is more difficult with formal withdrawal procedures in place. Consequently, RIOs with withdrawal clauses should be subject to fewer exit threats. Given that, in theory, there are two logics with different directionalities at play in theory, we only control for this institutional feature in the subsequent analysis. To capture the absence ('0') or presence ('1') of withdrawal clauses in the institutional design of RIO treaties in a given year, we coded the founding treaties and treaty changes, including primary law protocols and annexes of the 73 RIOs for the period between 1945 and 2022.

Studies on IO authority have made the point that besides pooling (see majority rule above), delegation is also an important feature for the functioning of IOs (Hooghe et al 2019b). Thus, we capture differences in delegation between organizations by whether a RIO has ('1') or lacks ('0') a regional court in a given year. The data stems from the ROCO dataset (see Panke et al 2020).

Should a crisis or an external shock arise, membership in a RIO with global powers might provide sheltering opportunities for member states in geopolitical, security-based or economic terms (Hey 2003, Ingebritsen et al 2006, Thorhallsson 2018). As these RIOs are especially important to their member states, exit threats might occur less often. We control whether or not a G20 state has been a member of a RIO at a given point in time to capture regional hegemon membership.

Another factor that might influence the general importance of a RIO as an outlet for regional cooperation for a specific state is regime complexity (Panke and Stapel 2018, Panke and Stapel 2025). The fewer alternative memberships a state has, the less likely are exit threats as the state lacks viable alternatives that could substitute for the respective RIO (Lipscy 2015). As such, in the age of regime complexity, all states that are members of more than one RIO could substitute membership in one RIO for another (Haftel and Hofmann 2019, Hofmann 2019, Alter 2022, Haftel and Lenz 2022, Daßler 2023, Langlet and Vadrot 2023). Although no single RIO includes all the policy areas or member states with which a given state may wish to cooperate, RIOs are nonetheless substitutable to the extent that the state could opt for reforms in alternative RIOs, including changes in the policy functions addressed, or seek to integrate other potentially relevant members. However, these types of reforms are potentially very difficult to achieve. In practice, RIOs' substitutability depends on the extent of their value differentiation (Henning and Pratt 2023, Pratt 2023). This is captured by the alternative venues of regional cooperation, based on the number of RIO memberships a state holds in a given year (calculated with ROCO 2.0 data on state membership in RIOs).

A contagion effect captures the decreasing political importance of an organization due to previous exits of member states (von Borzyskowski and Vabulas 2019b). In most RIOs, there is a one- or two-year time period between a state giving notice of its intention to exit and the actual withdrawal. Based on this procedural rule, we capture whether a state exit is contagious and triggers other states to issue threats to exit from the same organization during the three following years. We code the contagion variable with '1' if an important member state (measured by being in the top 25 percent of strong economic states within the RIO in question based on cumulative GDP) left during the three previous years and with '0' otherwise.

Finally, exit threats might be prevented or enhanced by overriding geopolitical conflict or crises. We measure interstate conflicts based on the UCDP/PRIO Armed Conflict Dataset version 24.1 (Gleditsch et al 2002). We code this variable as '1' if in a given year a state is in an interstate conflict (type 2 conflicts in the dataset) with another state with which it also shares membership in at least one RIO.

Furthermore, we run robustness checks. To this end, we replicate the models by using multilevel regressions (Table A.5). In addition to the policy scope covered by an IO based on its treaties, we also focus on the number of economic competencies and the number of security competencies as the two core functions of many RIOs. The data stems from the ROCO 2.0 dataset (see Panke et al 2020).

The unit of analysis is state-RIO-year. The dependent variable is binary in nature, with exit threats coded with '1', while '0' indicates that a state is a member of a RIO in a given year without making a threat to withdraw. As illustrated, there is a total of 123 exit threats (see Chapter Three). Methodologically, we follow King and Zeng (2001a, 2001b) and von Borzyskowski and Vabulas (2019b) in applying a rare event logistic regression analysis.[1] The standard errors are clustered on RIOs and years to take into account that we have repeated observations of RIOs over time so that country observations are not independent over time and within RIOs. All independent and control variables are lagged by two years and the models are kept parsimonious, avoiding multicollinearity.

Additionally, the insights from the quantitative analysis are complemented by qualitative narrative evidence in order to shed light on the mechanisms at play and provide contextual insights. The qualitative analysis is based on a multiplicity of sources in order to triangulate information. We draw on media sources, official RIO documents, and secondary literature. In addition, we conducted more than 150 interviews with RIO and state representatives as well as case or country experts. The interviews were semi-structured and took place virtually or in-person between February 2023 and April 2025.[2]

Empirical analysis

The regression analysis shows that the expectations concerning specific support in particular are empirically plausible. In comparison, diffuse support plays a minor role for the prevalence of exit threats (see Table 5.1).

Specific support

The first hypothesis focuses on the throughput component of Easton's systems theory and captures the role of specific support. It expects that the chances that a state's demands are generally turned into outputs in a RIO are influenced by country as well as organizational features and has implications for the chances of exit threats to take place in those instances in which the state inevitably fails to translate a specific input into a specific output.

Table 5.1 reveals that an increase in power of a state significantly reduces the chances for exit threats (models 1–4; see also Table A.5). In line with the literature that demonstrates that powerful states are better equipped compared to weaker

Table 5.1: Rare event regressions (controls omitted)

	Model 1	Model 2	Model 3	Model 4
Specific support				
Relative state power	−0.000***	−0.000**	−0.000***	−0.000**
	(0.000)	(0.000)	(0.000)	(0.000)
Relative ideological dissimilarity of state	0.170**	0.230**	0.166*	0.227**
	(0.084)	(0.091)	(0.090)	(0.098)
RIO majority rule	1.330****	1.358****	1.350****	1.386****
	(0.350)	(0.353)	(0.355)	(0.363)
RIO policy scope	0.017****	0.017****	0.018****	0.017****
	(0.005)	(0.005)	(0.005)	(0.005)
Diffuse support				
Socialization into cooperation	−0.124***		−0.124***	
	(0.041)		(0.041)	
Socialization into RIO	−0.009	−0.009		
	(0.009)	(0.009)		
RIO age			−0.007	−0.007
			(0.009)	(0.010)
RIO democracy		−0.061		−0.059
		(0.072)		(0.074)
With controls (omitted)				
Constant	−6.594****	−6.971****	−6.630****	−7.018****
	(0.744)	(0.923)	(0.753)	(0.943)
Observations	27826	27826	27826	27826
AIC	1351.04	1364.18	1351.26	1364.47

Note: Clustered standard errors in parentheses with *$p<0.1$, ** $p<0.05$, *** $p<0.01$, **** $p<0.001$

states to ensure that their positions are reflected in the IO's policies and decisions (Moravcsik 1998, Kuziemko and Werker 2006, Milewicz and Snidal 2016), this finding suggests that powerful members attribute more specific support to the RIO and are therefore less likely to voice threats to withdraw when they encounter a situation in which they did not succeed translating their inputs into outputs. Vice versa, weaker member states are less successful in influencing RIO outputs in general and consequently attribute less specific support to the organization that functions as a buffer preventing exit threats, which increases the prevalence of exit threats for weaker states.

This became evident in the case of ECOWAS. In light of the devastating civil wars in Liberia and Sierra Leone in the 1990s, it had also gained considerable competencies in the areas of peace and security as well as democracy protection (Yaya 2014, Ramanzini Júnior and Luciano 2020, Suzuki 2020a, 2020b). These developments were driven by powerful member states such as Cote d'Ivoire, Nigeria, and Senegal as they feared spillover effects from conflicts and regarded regional stability as a precondition for regional economic integration and development (Striebinger 2012, Hartmann and Striebinger 2015, Agbo et al 2018, Oshita and Alli 2021). Nevertheless, these powerful member states are also confronted with instances in which they are dissatisfied with the organization (Interview #55, 16/09/2024). In the case of Nigeria, this occurred over its opposition to the potential accession of Morocco (The Nation 2017) and perceived one-sided personnel decisions by the ECOWAS Commission (Sunday Trust 2022). However, Nigeria is also the undisputed regional hegemon in West Africa and the 'backbone' of the organization as 'without Nigeria there would not be a functioning ECOWAS' (Interview #55, 16/09/2024). As a result, ECOWAS 'definitely listens differently when powerful states complain' and 'there is a tendency to keep larger states content' (Interview #55, 16/09/2024). Accordingly, Nigeria has considerable influence in the organization and is able to ensure that its demands are reflected in the outputs produced by ECOWAS. This is exemplified by the organization's decision to construct the Chinese-financed headquarter buildings in Abuja, Nigeria's capital (Interview #55, 16/09/2024). Nigeria generally displays considerable specific support for ECOWAS, which creates a buffer against the voicing of exit threats in instances when it does not get what it wants.

In contrast, for smaller states, it is much more difficult to shape ECOWAS's decisions in line with their preferences (Interview #55, 16/09/2024). This reduces their specific support toward the organization and increases the chance that less powerful states resort to exit threats in specific situations. In 1999, Mauritania, dissatisfied with ECOWAS's plans to introduce a common currency (AFP 1999), resorted to an exit threat, which it eventually realized (Panafrican News Agency 2000; Interview #51, 12/09/2024). This underscores that while powerful states, being able to shape an organization's policy output in line with their preferences, have a 'buffer' in terms of specific support leading them to refrain from exit threats, this is not the case for less powerful states, which are more likely to threaten their withdrawal in situations when their grievances are not sufficiently addressed.

The regression analysis also reveals that ideological (dis)similarity is robustly positive and significant in all model specifications (see Table 5.1 and Table A.5). The greater the ideological divergence between a state and the other RIO member states, the higher the chances that this state voices an exit threat in the respective RIO. Ideological similarity is important for both strategies of states to exert influence in an organization: arguing and bargaining. For arguing, it serves as a common yardstick to evaluate the quality of arguments and renders cognitive shortcuts with positive evaluations more likely (Habermas 1995a, Risse 2000, Panke 2010c), while it reduces the distance of win-sets and is thus conducive to successful bargaining as well (Keohane 1984, Putnam 1988). The more dissimilar a state is ideologically compared to the other member states, the less likely it is that its inputs are translated into outputs, which increases the chances for exit threats. Conversely, if a state is ideologically close to the average RIO member, it is more probable that its inputs resonate within the RIO, reducing the likelihood of responses to instances of displeasure with exit threats.

Russia's threat to walk out of the OSCE in 2008 sheds light on the importance of ideological similarity. The OSCE – founded as the Conference on Security and Cooperation in Europe during the Cold War détente in 1975 – is the most comprehensive RIO in Europe in terms of membership, involving all independent European states, the former members of the Soviet Union, as well as the US and Canada (Panke et al 2020). The OSCE's work was initially organized around the three 'baskets' of security, economics, and humanitarian affairs, with the latter increasing in importance over time (Sandole 2007, Romano 2009). In this respect, the OSCE came to orient itself towards Western interpretations of democracy and human rights as well as multidimensional perspectives on security (Pourchot 2011, Mosser 2015). This Western dominance in the organization was also evident in an uneven distribution of posts (Ghebali 2005: 380). Over time, Russia and other post-Soviet member states ability to shift the organization's output according to their policy preferences – focused on traditional 'hard' security concerns in general – was decreasing (Stewart 2008: 270–1). More specifically, in 2006, their dissatisfaction was sparked by the work of the OSCE's Office for Democratic Institutions and Human Rights (ODIHR). Established in 1991, ODIHR played an important role in the OSCE's monitoring of elections (Sandole 2007). On this matter, in 2006, Russian Minister of Foreign Affairs Sergey Lavrov said he

> no longer saw the point of belonging to the Organisation for Security and Co-operation in Europe because the body had become pre-occupied with human rights. Mr Lavrov told delegates to the OSCE's annual meeting

in Brussels that if it did not concentrate its focus solely on security related initiatives, Russia and some of its former Soviet allies would consider withdrawing. (*Daily Telegraph* 2006).

This underlines the Russian perception that 'the OSCE has become an arena for certain forces to promote biased political decisions', which lead Russia to 'consider whether to continue being a member of this dubious organization' (WTPS 2008). In this regard, an official stated at that time that 'Russia hasn't handed over its sovereignty to anyone, and we're not ruled by a colonial government that might decide on our behalf what is democratic and what is not' (WTPS 2008). This is indicative of the stark ideological differences between Russia and the Western OSCE members (Warkotsch 2007). This was further evidenced by the fact that Russia regarded the OSCE as deploying double standards against those member states 'East of Vienna' (Ghebali 2005: 379), for example in terms of election monitoring. According to Russia, this created 'a de facto new line of division between "state subjects" and "state objects" – or, in other words, that the OSCE was turning into an organisation where a group of countries was able to teach lessons to and impose unilateral obligations upon all others' (Ghebali 2005: 379–80). Accordingly, Western member states of the OSCE 'accused Moscow of trying to "weaken" the OSCE in its role as a defender of democracy and electoral transparency' and of 'want[ing] to make it "less relevant"' (Qatar News Agency 2007). In effect, the ideological divergence from a large part of the (Western) member states of the OSCE reduced Russia's ability for successful communicative action, while the distance between the respective win-sets also made Russia's bargaining attempts more difficult. As a result, Russia found it more difficult to translate its demands into outputs of the organizations without resorting to exit threats.

Compared to the OSCE, Russia is ideologically more similar to the other member states of the EAEU. Founded in

2015 as the successor organization of the Eurasian Economic Community, the goal of the EAEU was to foster economic cooperation and integration in the post-Soviet realm, most importantly among the member states Belarus, Kazakhstan, Kyrgyzstan, Russia, and Tajikistan (Libman 2011, 2019). The organization had been created as result of a Russian initiative and Russia exercised considerable influence over its neighbors, with which it shared ideological similarities due to their authoritarian governance style and common history. Russia was therefore able to influence the EAEU's decision-making processes and its demands were generally reflected in the EAEU's output (Libman 2019), increasing Russia's specific support for the organization. This is not to say that Russia did not experience instances of dissatisfaction within the EAEU, most importantly due to the resistance of other member states to Russian-led integration initiatives. This was the case, for example, when the other member states, especially Belarus and Kazakhstan, resisted the introduction of a common electronic currency (Eurasia Diary 2019) and lagged behind in their efforts toward economic integration (Tajikistan Newsline 2021). However, due to greater specific support for the EAEU based on influence as a result of ideological similarities within the organization, Russia did not revert to exit threats.

Another example is Venezuela's withdrawal threat against the OAS. While being the oldest RIO in the Americas and the one with the most comprehensive membership, the OAS also has a very strong focus on democracy and human rights (Olivari 2014, Perina 2015, Stapel 2022). This is evident not just in the OAS's organizational motto 'more rights for more people' (OAS 2025), but also in the work of the IACHR, which is the paramount authority concerning human rights protection in the Americas. One of the mechanisms at the disposal of the IACHR are reports about the human rights situation in OAS members based on on-site visits by its staff (Interview #148, 13/02/2025). Venezuela in 2009 threatened to withdraw from the OAS, in reaction to such a report that heavily criticized the human rights situation in the country (EVN 2009), with Hugo Chávez stating: 'Let me make this official […]. If they convict us in the OAS or any of its bodies, Venezuela is pulling out, because it would make no sense to be there' (AFP 2007). Venezuela's anger was also a direct consequence of the fact that it regarded itself as being more severely scrutinized by the OAS, whereas human rights violations by the US, especially in its Guantanamo Bay military base, were ignored (AFP 2007). Due to ideological divergences with large parts of the OAS, and especially the US, which continues to yield significant influence within the organization, there are considerable discrepancies in terms of human rights considerations between Venezuela and other member states of the OAS, in particular the US (Ribeiro Hoffmann 2019). It was difficult for Venezuela to argue or bargain for its interests to be taken into account and its demands to be generally reflected in the organizations' output, increasing the chances that Venezuela resorts to an exit threat. In comparison, the situation was different when Venezuela's human rights situation was criticized by MERCOSUR, where human rights and democracy also played an important role (Ramanzini Júnior and Luciano 2020). After the death of Chávez in 2013 and the transfer of power to Nicolás Maduro, the democracy and human rights situation in Venezuela deteriorated (Ribeiro 2022). MERCOSUR had admitted Venezuela as a member in 2012 and the other member states soon began to criticize the worsening democracy and human rights situation in the country (Reisdoerfer and Castillo 2022). At a MERCOSUR meeting, the Brazilian Minister of Foreign Affairs stated: 'We are saying: Stop with this! Enough with the deaths, enough with the repression. It is not possible to inflict such torture on the people' (Reuters 2017). Having suspended Venezuela in 2016 over the non-fulfillment of treaty obligations related to economic integration, the following year MERCOSUR explicitly suspended Venezuela due to undemocratic governance and human rights violations by the Maduro regime (VOA News 2017, Reisdoerfer and Castillo

2022, Siman 2023). Venezuela was highly dissatisfied with this situation and strongly rejected the suspension, which it even labelled a 'coup at the heart of Mercosur' (Voice of America 2016). MERCOSUR is comprised solely of South American countries and is characterized by greater ideological similarity than is the case for the OAS, which also includes North American member states, primarily the US and Canada (Caballero Santos 2013, Briceño-Ruiz and Ribeiro Hoffmann 2015, Weiffen 2017). Venezuela was generally accustomed to being able to shape MERCOSUR's outputs according to its demands and displayed greater specific support toward the organization in comparison to the OAS. Thus, while MERCOSUR arguably took a much more confrontational stance against Venezuela compared to the OAS, Venezuela did not threaten to withdraw from MERCOSUR.

Both Russia and Venezuela are distinctively dissimilar in terms of their ideological leanings in comparison to the respective majority of OSCE and OAS members, respectively, which reduced their ability to transform their inputs into outputs in these organizations, undergirding their expressions of dissatisfaction in the form of exit threats. At the same time, when these states encountered a situation in which they were discontent with RIOs with which they had greater ideational similarity and attributed greater specific support to them, due to being able to shape policy outcomes in line with their interests, both states refrained from issuing threats to withdraw. Next to country features, the chances that a member state is able to prevent that its demands are not sufficiently reflected in outputs can be influenced by organizational factors. This includes the extent of pooled authority and a RIO's policy scope.

Concerning the effect of pooling in RIOs' decision-making, the quantitative analysis reveals that in RIOs with majority rule the likelihood of exit threats increases significantly (Table 5.1, models 1–4; see also Table A.5), which is also supported by narrative evidence. An example of such a mechanism at play is the 2010 exit threat of Nicaragua in the OAS, which came to bear in the context of a border dispute in association with allegations of sovereignty violations leveled by Costa Rica against Nicaragua (Rudall 2018). In October 2010, Costa Rica claimed that its western neighbor's dredging of a canal connecting the San Juan River with a wetland nearby constituted a breach of the boundary established under the Cañas-Jerez Treaty of Limits (Cogan 2016, Müller 2018). It then called upon the OAS to get involved in the mediation of the dispute in order to have Nicaragua remove its troops from the border area (OAS 2010), with the Permanent Council of the OAS adopting a resolution on the situation in the border area:

> The OAS approved a resolution on Friday calling for [the] removal of Nicaraguan soldiers and security forces from the disputed area along the San Juan River, prompting Costa Rica to declare a 'diplomatic victory.' In his response, Ortega said his government was considering withdrawing from the OAS and he called the OAS permanent council's vote 'manipulated' and 'a conspiracy'. (Inside Costa Rica 2010)

In majority-based organizations, individual states can be potentially outvoted on contentious issues, which can lead to dissatisfaction with the RIO – and the threat to withdraw from the organization – should a state's interests systematically be ignored by fellow member states. This was also evident in the case of Venezuela and the OAS. As outlined earlier, since the beginning of the presidency of Nicolas Maduro in 2013, Venezuela had experienced steep declines in terms of economic development, democracy, and human rights (Siman 2023). These developments increasingly attracted criticism from the OAS (Ribeiro Hoffmann 2019; Interview #149, 14/03/2025). For instance, in 2016 OAS Secretary General Luis Almagro said that 'Maduro's government had violated basic democratic principles, which had altered the constitutional order of the country' and that the 'situation facing Venezuela today is the direct result of the actions of those currently in power' (*The Guardian* 2016). As a consequence of the organization's critique against democratic backsliding and the deteriorating human rights situation (Associated Press 2017, Ribeiro Hoffmann 2019), in 2017 Venezuela 'threatened to withdraw [...] if the bloc held a meeting on the South American country's crisis without approval', while also 'suggesting it [the OAS] is a puppet of the U.S. government' (UPI 2017). As both the OAS's General Assembly and Permanent Council adopt decisions by two-thirds majority, Venezuela could neither prevent that its domestic political situation was repeatedly placed on the organization's agenda, nor the passing of critical resolutions (Interview #148, 13/03/2025, Interview #149, 14/03/2025; OAS 2018). Being unable to influence the OAS's policy outputs in line with its demands on numerous occasions, Venezuela lacked specific support for the organization, which increased the chances of it reverting to an exit threat (UPI 2017). As a result, Venezuela threatened to withdraw from OAS in 2017.

The negative effects of majority voting on states' specific support toward a RIO are also evident in the CoE. In January 2024, PACE voted against ratifying the credentials of the Azerbaijani delegation, thereby effectively excluding it from participating in the assembly's proceedings for the entire year (Interview #95, 29/01/2025). While Azerbaijan had long been a 'problematic' member state of the CoE, this decision was speficially the result of human rights violations by the Azerbaijani government, especially in the context of Azerbaijani aggression against Nagorno Karabakh in the summer of 2023, as well as the refusal by the Azerbaijani government to admit CoE election observers into the country (Ailincai 2024; Interview #95, 29/01/2025). As one CoE official noted, 'there are three things that Azerbaijan is not doing well: they take political prisoners. They force Armenian Karabakh's to leave. And they do not allow our Rapporteur to visit Azerbaijan or to monitor the elections. And on that basis, [PACE] took this decision' (Interview #12, 08/02/2024).

Being naturally opposed to this measure but unable to prevent it due to PACE taking decisions by majority vote (Interview #95, 29/01/2025), Azerbaijan reacted by threatening to terminate its membership in the CoE. President Ilham Aliyev 'said that his country may consider withdrawing entirely from the Council of Europe if the rights of its delegation are not restored within a year' (Anadolu Agency 2024). This highlights that if states have reduced opportunities to shape a RIO's outputs according to their demands due to the organization's majority-based decision-making, their specific support is reduced, which in turn increases their incentives to revert to exit threats.

The expectation for the second institutional design feature is also supported by empirical evidence: The broader a RIO's scope of policy competencies, the more policy issues member states can potentially disagree about and be potentially harmed by. Accordingly, the chances that discontent cannot be generally addressed in the throughput process of a RIO increases with a broader set of an organization's policy mandates, which also makes exit threats more likely. In line with this expectation, the policy scope of organizations has a robustly positive, significant effect on the likelihood of withdrawal threats to occur (Table 5.1, models 1–4, Table A.5). The same applies for the scope of economic competencies and security competencies (see Table A.6 in the Appendix). A broader policy scope also implies that such RIOs can receive multiple withdrawal threats relating to different issues. One such example is the EAEU, which is equipped with 126 policy competencies across different fields (Libman 2019, Panke et al 2020, Gast 2023). This entails the risk that member states are unable to ensure the incorporation of their demands in the organization's outputs cooperation across a wide variety of policy issues, which may then reduce their specific support and make exit threats more likely. In the EAEU, this becomes evident in a high density of exit threats. For instance, Kazakhstan and Kyrgyzstan each threatened to withdraw due to the EAEU's trade and single market policies. While 'Kazakh suppliers constantly complain[ed] about unjust Russian restrictions on transit supplies or the re-export of products under sanctions, in particular Kazakh coal for Ukraine' (BBC 2020a), Kyrgyzstan did 'not like the fact that the EAEU project, attractive for it, first of all, as a single market, turned out to be a closed market' (D & S 2020). Moreover in 2018, Belarus took issue with geopolitical and security stances of the EAEU and 'threatened that the country will withdraw from the EAEU if Minsk's position was not heard' (Country Watch 2020). In contrast, this is not the case for the Commonwealth of Independent States (CIS), which was founded primarily as a political project by Russia to exert control over the post-Soviet space (Libman 2011). While CIS displays significant membership overlap with the EAEU (Libman and Obydenkova 2020), it is equipped with a much more limited number of policy competencies, reducing the likelihood that member states accumulate dissatisfaction across a wide range of policy areas. Member states therefore display greater specific support for CIS, which has not been subjected to a comparable number of exit threats.

In sum, the analysis has revealed that specific support plays a strong and important role to account for variation in the prevalence of exit threats in and between RIOs. An increase in specific support reduces the chances that a state, when inevitably encountering a situation in which its demands were not reflected in a RIO's output, voices its discontent in the form of exit threats. Hypothesis 1 outlined country and organizational features that impact whether a member state is generally able to influence a RIO's output in line with its demands, generating specific support of a specific organization and reducing the likelihood for exit threats. There is empirical support for the relevance of ideological similarity reducing the likelihood of withdrawal threats. Hence, exit threats are more prevalent with states that differ strongly in ideological terms from their fellow RIO members, as was the case for Russia in the OSCE and Venezuela in the OAS. By contrast, states matching the ideological orientation of the other member states closely, such as Russia in the EAEU and Venezuela in

MERCOSUR, are less likely to voice threats to withdraw. Likewise, RIOs characterized by high internal heterogeneity attract less specific support and are more likely to be subject to exit threats than more homogenous organizations. Also, the empirical analysis shows that relative power decreases the chances of exit threats in those instances in which a powerful state fails to translate a specific demand in a specific RIO output, as was the case with Nigeria, which, even though it was discontent with certain personnel decisions by the ECOWAS Commission, is generally very much able to ensure that the organization's policy output aligns with its demands, resulting in specific support for the RIO.

Next to these country features, the prevalence of exit threats is also influenced by organizational features for specific support. As expected, RIOs with majority rule have in-built provisions to outvote member states, which – especially if the same state(s) are systematically in the minority – reduce specific support and create grounds to voice grievances in the form of exit threats. The examples of Venezuela in the OAS and Azerbaijan in the CoE illustrate that if states are unable to prevent unfavorable decisions by failing to influence the RIO's outputs according to their demands, this provides them with incentives to threaten their withdrawal from the organization. Finally, a narrow policy scope reduces the scope of possible demands towards the RIO and limits the grounds for potential dissatisfaction, which would otherwise have reduced specific support. Overall, RIOs with broader policy scopes have a greater propensity for exit threats compared to organizations that focus on a few policy fields only. This became evident in the large number of exit threats occurring in the EAEU compared to CIS, whereby the former organization covers a much broader array of issue areas than the latter.

Diffuse support

Diffuse support for a political system produces commitment and can buffer temporal dissatisfactions including in the throughput stage and is for that reason expected to reduce the prevalence of exit threats. There are two drivers of diffuse support: socialization and democracy, which operate on both the country and the organizational level.

While the empirical analysis has provided systematic evidence for the specific support hypothesis, the findings concerning diffuse support are nuanced. All covariates point into the expected direction, yet only one driver has the expected significant effect: the level of democracy of a state in question. Compared to specific support, the role of diffuse support for the prevalence of exit threats within and between RIOs is less stringent.

Based on the theoretical discussion, we expect that a state's socialization into the value of cooperation also plays a role. Accordingly, autocracies are expected to use withdrawal threats more frequently than their more democratic counterparts as the latter are more strongly socialized into placing value in cooperation as well as into political practices of alternating winning and losing as well as compromising, which builds up diffuse support towards cooperation in RIOs. In line with this expectation, an increase in democracy significantly reduces the chances of threats to withdraw from RIOs being voiced (Table 5.1, models 1–4; see also Table A.5 in the Appendix). This fits the notion that democratic leaders are likely to be accustomed to political controversies between government and opposition and, due to their socialization, bound to accept compromise and majority decisions, whereas autocratic leaders are more likely to expect to get their way (Russett 1995, Brown et al 1996, Owen 1996). The narrative evidence further suggests that autocratic governments are likely to voice such threats when being unable to secure their individual interests in the throughput stage, for instance by preventing a RIO from a specific activity, statement or policy. Instances of outright rejection of criticism and associated expectations of non-interference thereby tie back to unfamiliarity with political controversies or the need for compromise in the realm of domestic politics for authoritarian leaders. In general, such behavior could be seen as indicative of a lack of compromise culture and the absence of socialization to norms associated with democracy among authoritarian member states.

This became evident in the EAEU, where members voiced nine withdrawal threats over a period of just six years (2014–20). Featuring Russia as well as several post-Soviet states (Belarus, Kazakhstan, and Kyrgyzstan), the EAEU is comprised exclusively of autocratically governed member states (Obydenkova and Libman 2019). As member states are not used to compromise and collective decision-making, they display lower diffuse support toward the EAEU. Disputes between member states regularly escalate into exit threats. For instance, Kyrgyzstan threatened to withdraw from the organization in 2017 over a border crossing dispute with fellow EAEU member Kazakhstan (BBC 2017). Previously, Belarussian President Lukashenko had voiced an exit threat over the lack of adherence to economic agreements within the EAEU (ARMINFO 2015). The empirical analysis further shows that when autocratic leaders are criticized by a RIO, for example due to their interference in elections or other violations against good governance standards, the chances of exit threats increase. A case in point is President Robert Mugabe's 2013 threat of withdrawing Zimbabwe from SADC. Having come into power in the early 1980s, by 2013 Mugabe had ruled Zimbabwe for about 30 years in an increasingly authoritarian way. Being unaccustomed to opposition as well as checks and balances or, in other words, fundamental principles of rules-based institutionalized multilateral governance, an official noted that Mugabe took

> the posture that [...] it's actually an incredible thing when Zimbabwe is criticized by SADC, it's like they cannot believe it, that that can happen because the default is that you should never criticize us. And they get shocked and offended when that happens, they don't expect it. And

> I think that was one instance when Mugabe was lashing out. (Interview #126, 14/02/2025)

President Mugabe's diffuse support for SADC was very limited and did not prevent him from threatening to withdraw from the organization when becoming dissatisfied with it (Interview #120, 12/02/2025). A similar situation occured in the PIF. Commodore Frank Bainimarama had come to power in Fiji in 2006 by means of a military coup and had henceforth ruled the country autocratically (Alley 2010). In response, the other PIF members continued to pressure Fiji for immediate democratic elections and opposed Bainimarama's reforms of the electoral system (The Australian 2008; Interview #78, 29/10/2024). As a result, in 2008, Bainimarama boycotted a PIF summit meeting and 'threatened to withdraw Fiji from the forum if it continued to oppose his plans to change the country's electoral system' (The Financial Times 2008).

Another example can be found in 1982 with regard to (then) autocratically ruled Turkey in the CoE. In 1980, the military, led by General Kenan Evren, took power in Turkey through a coup d'état (Soyaltin-Colella 2020). These events were heavily criticized by the CoE, with the possible expulsion of Turkey from the organization being mooted (Steiner 1982). In 1982, Evren threatened to withdraw from the organization as a response to the CoE's undue interference in Turkey's internal affairs. As PACE had passed a resolution condemning human rights violations by the Turkish military junta (Associated Press 1982a, BBC 2015), junta leader Evren warned of a 'decisive and definitive' reaction in case the CoE and its member states 'convert their interests in the developments in Turkey into interference in our internal affairs' (Associated Press 1982b).

Taken together, due to a lack of socialization into democratic procedures, oversight, and compromises, the diffuse support of authoritarian states for RIOs is more limited, making them more likely to revert to exit threats.

With respect to diffuse support generated via socialization into the RIO, we would expect that being a member in a specific organization for a longer period of time creates commitment and reduces a state's propensity to issue withdrawal threats. The regression analysis shows that an increase in membership duration indeed robustly reduces the chances for exits threats to occur in all model specifications. However, this effect is not significant in any of the four models for any of the significance thresholds (see Table 5.1). Narrative evidence further underlines that socialization through long membership duration is not sufficient to prevent states from threatening to withdraw – and realizing their threat – if they encounter situations in which their dissatisfaction with the RIO in question is not remedied. The Central European Initiative (CEI) is a case in point. It was founded in 1989 by Austria, Hungary, Italy, and Yugoslavia. Over time it increased in size to include 18 members from Central Eastern, South Eastern, and Eastern Europe (CEI 2023; Wästfelt and Pibernik 2017). CEI members cooperated in a wide range of mostly technical issue areas intended to bring (potential) candidate states closer to EU membership (Interview #2, 07/02/2023). Austria had regarded the CEI as a mostly ineffective and decreasingly relevant instrument for achieving these goals, especially the integration of the Western Balkan states into the EU (Interview #3, 22/02/2023). However, since the CEI as 'an Austrian-Italian foundation […] was one of the oldest regional organizations that ever existed for this region', it was 'not an easy decision' to consider withdrawing from the RIO (Interview #3, 22/02/2023). By contrast, while many non-founding CEI members had long been dissatisfied with the allocation of the organization's Secretary General and Alternate Secretary General posts to Italy and Austria, respectively, none of them had so far reverted to exit threats (Interview #2, 07/02/2023). More broadly, exit threats by long-time or even founding members of RIOs are no exception, as exemplified by the withdrawal threats of the US toward NATO and

Venezuela toward OAS (both 69 membership years), Nigeria toward ECOWAS (more than 42 membership years), the UK toward the EU (more than 39 membership years), Qatar toward the GCC (36 membership years), or Brazil toward MERCOSUR (25 membership years). The potential of socialization into an organization over time has also sometimes been overestimated by RIOs themselves. An example of this is the CoE, which, after the end of the Cold War, featured several not fully democratic countries emerging from the Soviet Union, including Russia and the Southern Caucasus states (Drezemczewski and Dzehtsiarou 2018). With regards to Russia, one CoE official stated:

> We invited countries to join the Democratic Club, we set up a full-time European Court of Human Rights, etc. The price to pay for this is we have countries that do not fully respect human rights, and we know that Russia was invited not because they *were* willing and able but because there was a *likelihood* that they would be able to actually be willing and able [...] If they're not part of the system, there's no way in which we could influence them. That's the basic premise. (Interview #15, 27/02/2024).

With the benefit of hindsight after the full-scale Russian invasion of Ukraine in 2022, this underpins the possibility that – at the height of the liberal moment in the 1990s and 2000s – the socializing effects of membership in international organizations may not just have been overestimated by IR scholars (Alderson 2001, Checkel 2004, Kelley 2004, Bearce and Bondanella 2007, Greenhill 2010), but also by (regional) IOs and the people working within them. This increasing disillusionment with the CoE's capacity to socialize Russia into democratic norms was also noted by another interviewee:

> [In] 2019, it was almost 25 years after [the Russian] accession, I was telling them, look, there is something

wrong because you are a country under the monitoring system for 25 years. The monitoring system in the [Parliamentary] Assembly was open to new member states. Are you still a new member state 25 years after? Something is wrong, something is very wrong. Because this monitoring position lasts for three, five years, finished. And then some decisions have to be taken, in or out. [...] If you are under monitoring [...] for 25 years, there is something wrong in the system. (Interview #16, 13/03/2024)

In effect, based on quantitative and qualitative insights, there is insufficient support for the notion that a long duration of membership in itself contributes to socialization processes that generate diffuse support to an extent that reduces the likelihood of exit threats when grievances occur.

When it comes to organizational features as drivers of diffuse support, Table 5.1 reveals that the coefficients for RIO age (socialization) and RIO democracy have the expected negative signs but are not significant in any of the models (see also Table A.5 in the Appendix).

The longer RIOs exist, the more time they have to socialize their member states and the greater the commitment of these states to the organization in question, which reduces the chances that states react to unaddressed grievances with exit threats. Comparing younger with older RIOs, we would have expected that the latter experience – *ceteris paribus* – fewer exit threats than the former. However, this is not supported by empirical evidence. The quantitative analysis shows that the RIO age lacks significance in all models (Table 5.1, Table A.5 in the Appendix).

Likewise, the qualitative analysis suggests that the age of a RIO is not a driver for diffuse support and does not, consequently, reduce the propensity of exit threats. As outlined above, long-time or founding members often threaten to withdraw from RIOs, and this can also happen after organizations have been in existence for long periods of time. While the withdrawal threats of the US toward NATO in 2018 and Venezuela toward OAS in 2017 occurred in year 69 of the organizations' respective existence, when the UK first threatened to withdraw from the EU in 2012, the organization and its predecessor had already been in existence for 61 years. ECOWAS had existed for 42 years when Nigeria first threatened to quit the organization in 2017, and Qatar in 2017 threatened to withdraw from the GCC during the RIO's 36th year of existence.

While these organizations had also experienced exit threats at earlier points in time, the example of PIF demonstrates that relatively old RIOs can also face hitherto unheard surges in exit threats. PIF, after experiencing just three exit threats during the first half century of its existence, in 2020 and 2021 suffered ten instances of member states threatening to withdraw from the organization. This indicates that, just as the mere duration of a state's membership, a RIO existing for a longer period of time does not necessarily guarantee socialization processes among its member states that contribute to diffuse support to an extent that would prevent them from reverting to exit threats.

Shifting the emphasis towards the last potential driver of diffuse support, RIO democracy, the quantitative analysis features the expected sign, but the findings are not significant at any of the levels (Table 5.1, models 1–4; see also Table A.5 in the Appendix). Therefore, we cannot conclude that more democratic RIOs obtain higher levels of diffuse support and have a lower likelihood of becoming subject to exit threats. Both democratic organizations, such as NATO, NAFTA, the EU, MERCOSUR, or PIF, and exclusively authoritarian RIOs, such as the GCC, LAS, or the EAEU have experienced exit threats. This speaks to scholarship on liberal script contestations, which argues that democracies place value on individual freedoms, including freedom of expression, rendering contestations through their members legitimate (Börzel et al 2024a, Börzel et al 2024b). Hence, in democratic RIOs, member state contestations are not regarded as illegitimate, increasing the chances for severe contestations in the form of exit threats.

Summing up, hypothesis 2 expects that the more a state is socialized towards cooperation in (regional) IOs, the greater its diffuse support for the RIO and the less likely it is to resort to threats to withdraw. This expectation holds concerning the socialization into democratic norms as autocratic states are more prone to voice displeasure by issuing exit threats compared to democratic states. Yet, the duration of membership, RIO age, and the democratic nature of organizations do not have a similar socializing effect, as evidenced by the case of the UK's threats to withdraw from the EU at the beginning of the 2010s, after about 40 years of membership in this rather old and democratic organization (Laffan and Telle 2023).

The added value of Easton's systems theory for the study of exit threats

Taken together, Easton's systems theory provides a valuable analytical lens to shed light on the multicausal phenomenon of exit threats in RIOs. Which demand a specific state brings as input into the political system at a given point in time is contingent and can vary over time, between states, and across issues. Some states might seek to address or resolve a particular economic or security problem, others might push for a specific policy, for instance in the form of secondary law (such as resolutions, regulations, directives or decisions) or activity (such as providing free trade zones, effective border control or other specific public goods and services), and yet other member states might seek to prevent policies or activities of RIOs as they seek symbolic legitimation or autocratic stability from the organization rather than any policy-related outputs. The outputs produced by RIOs are contingent – just as their evaluation by the respective states is idiosyncratic.

Irrespective of the nature and content of the specific demand, the chances for individual states to exert influence in the throughput stage and translate their specific demands into outputs in general generates specific support for the political system. Such general specific support, in turn, reduces the chances of exit threats in individual instances in which a state's grievances cannot be addressed sufficiently in the RIO's policy-making process. Conversely, if a state is not able to ensure that its core inputs are generally reflected into RIO outputs, dissatisfaction builds up while specific support gets reduced and withdrawal threats become increasingly likely. The empirical analysis shows that the chances for generalized individual influence in the throughput phase are impacted by country and institutional design features. Greater ideological dissimilarity, lower state power, broader policy scope, and the presence of majority voting reduce a state's general shaping ability and specific support, which increases the likelihood of exit threats.

As specific support for a political system can vary among members, political systems also require *diffuse support* to function – especially in the long run. Diffuse support is independent of policy or activity-related output of a RIO but rather based on general normative or ideational features attributed to the organization. Empirically, the analysis shows that only one country-factor source of diffuse support, in the form of democratic socialization, plays a role in reducing the propensity of exit threats from RIOs. Governments of democratic states are more socialized into placing value in principles such as rule-based governance, legitimate dissent, as well as the democratic logic of compromise and varying majority–minority patterns, according to which they belong to the winning side at one point in time, and to the losing side at another. In effect, democratic states are more inclined than autocracies to generally attribute diffuse support to political systems in which they, at times, fail to exert influence during the throughput phase. Thus, they are less likely to voice threats to withdraw.

With respect to RIOs, specific and diffuse support can delimit exit threats. Yet, specific support plays a major role in this respect, with four different drivers having influence, while the role of diffuse support is limited in nature. In other words, the resilience of RIOs tends to be mainly based on specific support, while only those RIOs in which the average level of democracy is high can also rely on diffuse support as a buffer preventing states from escalating grievances into exit threats.

Potential generalizations to other types of IOs

The empirical examination of the hypotheses concerning specific and diffuse support revealed that exit threats are more prevalent the fewer chances an individual state has to generally influence RIOs' throughput processes that transform demands into outputs. This is the case if a state is less powerful, if it is ideologically different from the other RIO members, if the organization is based on majority rule, and if the organization has a broad scope of policy competencies. In addition, the lower a state's overall commitment toward an organization based on democratic socialization, the more likely exit threats are. By the same token, when states attribute specific support to a RIO, as they are generally in a good position to make their interests heard, they tend to refrain from exit threats in situations in which they could not successfully translate their demands into RIO outputs. This is the case for strong states, states that are in ideological terms similar to the other member states, for RIOs with consensus rule decision-making, and for organizations with narrow policy scopes. Similarly, the chances for exit threats decrease when states attribute diffuse support to an organization, which is, however, in RIOs only the case for democratic states. Moreover, specific and diffuse support are not mutually exclusive, but complementary in nature, and exit threats are not voiced in every instance of dissatisfaction, as insufficient specific support can be compensated by diffuse support and the other way round. Considering the manifoldness of potential reasons for dissatisfaction (see Chapter Two) and given that unresolved grievances can persist – even for powerful and ideologically similar states – in consensus-oriented RIOs with narrow policy scopes specific support does not render diffuse support irrelevant or vice versa.

To what extent insights about the role of diffuse and specific support in shaping the prevalence of exit threats concerning RIOs apply to other types of IOs remains an open question, warranting further empirical investigation. Yet, based on the empirical analysis conducted for RIOs, some preliminary outlooks can be formulated (see also 'Applying Easton's theory to different types of IOs' in Chapter Four).

Firstly, RIOs as community organizations theoretically represent least likely cases for exit threats in IOs. Yet, based on the factors that the empirical analysis identified as relevant for exit threats to become increasingly prevalent, global IOs should feature a slightly lower rate of exit threats than RIOs. As they tend to have a more limited policy scope than RIOs, which reduces the prevalence of exit threats, they tend to be subject to greater ideological divergence and greater power asymmetry with many weak states, resulting in more limited specific support. In contrast, as Table 5.2 illustrates, the size of an IO has no significant effect in itself, suggesting that global IOs, which are generally larger in size, cannot per se be expected to be more often contested by exit threats. However, when global IOs, due to their larger membership, feature states that are in interstate conflicts with one another, a spillover into the IO and contestations in this realm linked to potential side taking is possible, which would lead to the expectation of an increase in exit threats (see Table 5.2).

Secondly, with respect to democratic and autocratic IOs, autocratic IOs should feature more exit threats than democratic IOs. However, the insights from the empirical analysis of RIOs suggest that the differences between both types of IO might not be as pronounced as theoretically expected (see 'Applying Easton's theory to different types of IOs' in Chapter Four). Only the democratic socialization of states has a significant

Table 5.2: Rare event regressions (controls shown)

	Model 1	Model 2	Model 3	Model 4
Specific support				
Relative state power	−0.000***	−0.000**	−0.000***	−0.000**
	(0.000)	(0.000)	(0.000)	(0.000)
Relative ideological dissimilarity of state	0.170**	0.230**	0.166*	0.227**
	(0.084)	(0.091)	(0.090)	(0.098)
RIO majority rule	1.330****	1.358****	1.350****	1.386****
	(0.350)	(0.353)	(0.355)	(0.363)
RIO policy scope	0.017****	0.017****	0.018****	0.017****
	(0.005)	(0.005)	(0.005)	(0.005)
Diffuse support				
Socialization into cooperation	−0.124***		−0.124***	
	(0.041)		(0.041)	
Socialization into RIO	−0.009	−0.009		
	(0.009)	(0.009)		
RIO age			−0.007	−0.007
			(0.009)	(0.010)
RIO democracy		−0.061		−0.059
		(0.072)		(0.074)
Controls				
RIO withdrawal clause	−0.137	−0.140	−0.126	−0.132
	(0.346)	(0.353)	(0.333)	(0.342)
RIO size	−0.013	−0.014	−0.013	−0.014
	(0.014)	(0.014)	(0.013)	(0.013)

(continued)

Table 5.2: Rare event regressions (controls shown) (continued)

	Model 1	Model 2	Model 3	Model 4
RIO court	0.121	0.045	0.100	0.028
	(0.374)	(0.372)	(0.367)	(0.366)
Previous exits	−1.504	−1.469	−1.502	−1.469
	(1.066)	(1.059)	(1.072)	(1.067)
Interstate conflicts	1.300*	1.366*	1.300*	1.363*
	(0.747)	(0.759)	(0.746)	(0.759)
Regional hegemon	−0.084	−0.157	−0.015	−0.089
	(0.339)	(0.364)	(0.362)	(0.388)
Regime complexity	0.075	0.088	0.068	0.081
	(0.102)	(0.109)	(0.101)	(0.108)
Constant	−6.594****	−6.971****	−6.630****	−7.018****
	(0.744)	(0.923)	(0.753)	(0.943)
Observations	27826	27826	27826	27826
AIC	1351.04	1364.18	1351.26	1364.47

Note: Clustered standard errors in parentheses with *$p<0.1$, ** $p<0.05$, *** $p<0.01$, **** $p<0.001$

effect, while the overall democratic nature of the organization is not significant.

Thirdly, concerning rule-setting/standard-setting and activity-centered/operational IOs, the theoretical expectation has been that the latter is task-specific and should thus receive a more limited number of exit threats than the other type of IOs, consisting of a mix of general purpose and task specific organizations (see 'Applying Easton's theory to different types of IOs' in Chapter Four). Given that the empirical analysis of RIOs revealed that organizations with narrow policy scopes have a more limited propensity for exit threats compared to organizations with broader sets of policy competencies, the

ACCOUNTING FOR THE VARYING PREVALENCE OF EXIT THREATS

empirical expectation would also be that activity-centered/operational IOs should attract fewer exit threats.

Fourthly, IOs can differ concerning the extent of legalization (Abbott et al 2000), which is especially prevalent in US-led compared to China-led IOs. Table 5.2 also controls for the presence or absence of regional courts. Interestingly, delegation in the form of the presence of a regional court has a systematically positive effect on the prevalence of threats to withdraw but is not significant in any of the models. Qualitative evidence accentuates that some states are explaining their threats to withdraw from an organization with reference to RIO courts' cases and judgements.[3] In some instances, countries justified their exit threats by questioning the authority of a RIO's court. For instance, Costa Rica protested with a withdrawal threat against the judgment of the Central American Court of Justice (CACJ) in 2012 in SICA:

> Costa Rica has rejected a ruling by [CACJ], which claims that the country has caused environmental damage due to a 160km road which runs parallel to the San Juan River. [...] Costa Rica has even threatened to withdraw from the SICA, whilst Nicaragua holds the presidency at this authority. The case against Costa Rica was filed by the Nicaraguan National Recycling Forum [...] as well as the Nicaraguan Foundation for Sustainable Development [...], in December 2011. Costa Rican President Laura Chinchilla has called the CACJ decision spurious and illegal and it *does not recognise this court as an authority*, especially given that its headquarters are based in Nicaragua. (Inside Costa Rica 2010, emphasis added)

While in some instances individual states are protesting against adverse court judgments by voicing exit threats vis-à-vis the corresponding RIO, not all regional courts are equally active and equally likely to take a clear stance against a member state (compare Alter 2014 with Panke 2010b). This finding may also be applicable to global and other types of IOs. It would lead to the expectation that the degree of legalization does not influence dynamics of internal contestation and member state grievances as such. Whenever an IO has a court on paper only, such instances cannot bring about a state's disappointment with the court and are thus unlikely to generate threats to exit the organization.

Finally, comparing China-led and US-led IOs to IOs without global powers, one might expect that states refrain from exit threats in the former but not the latter organizations, as the other member states can shelter in the wake of crises and external challenges and are disincentivized from issuing threats to exit such valuable organizations.[4] However, states may also refrain from issuing exit threats due to fear of retaliation by global powers.[5] Yet, the quantitative analysis of RIOs suggests that there is no significant effect (see Table 5.2, models 1–4). This suggests that China-led and US-led IOs should not per se be expected to be less contested when compared to IOs without global power membership.

SIX

Conclusions

This chapter summarizes the main findings concerning the role of specific and diffuse support as drivers of exit threats, discusses the linkages between withdrawal threats and actual exits and outlines avenues for future research.

Talking the talk of exit threats

In previous years, contestations of the LIO and the (regional) IOs underpinning it have been extensively studied (Hooghe et al 2019a, Deitelhoff and Zimmermann 2020, Eilstrup-Sangiovanni and Hofmann 2020, Börzel and Zürn 2021, Lake et al 2021, Dijkstra et al 2025). Recent research has analyzed the underlying reasons for the contestation of IOs (Kreuder-Sonnen and Rittberger 2023, Heinkelmann-Wild et al 2024a, Kreuder-Sonnen and Zangl 2024), IOs' strategies in responding to these challenges (Hirschmann 2021, Schmidtke and Lenz 2023) and different forms of contestation of IOs through their member states (Kreuder-Sonnen and Zangl 2016, Kruck et al 2022, Daßler et al 2024) – including withdrawals (von Borzyskowski and Vabulas 2019b). Withdrawal threats have received less attention. While von Borzyskowski and Vabulas (2023) exploratively analyzed the effectiveness of exit threats in achieving IO internal reforms, the analysis presented in this book shifts the focus and investigates the factors contributing to their occurrence in the first place. This is relevant, as threats to withdraw have potentially severe consequences for IOs: even if not realized through actual withdrawals, exit threats differ from other forms of internal contestation: by linking critique and demands to the possibility of discontinuing RIO membership, they put into question the legitimacy and value of the IO as such – and whether the continued operation of the IO is relevant at all. Calling an IO into question can create shock waves, raising fears of the demise (Gray 2018, Eilstrup-Sangiovanni 2020, 2021, Debre and Dijkstra 2021, Dijkstra and Debre 2022, Mumby 2023) or disintegration of the RIO (Gänzle 2019, Walter 2021, Haftel and Nadel 2024, Schmidt 2024) among the remaining member states. This was evident in the case of Trump's exit threat towards NATO (Schuessler and Shifrinson 2019, Sperling and Webber 2019, Schuette 2021) and the withdrawal threats of several Micronesian states against PIF in 2020 and 2021 (Schleich 2021, *The Guardian* 2022b, Panke et al 2024). Constituting potentially negative implications for RIOs' effectiveness, legitimacy, and resilience (Nolte and Mijares 2022, Ribeiro Hoffmann 2020), in this book we analyzed the varying prevalence of exit threats based on a complete sample of RIOs as a subtype of IOs.

In order to add insights as to why RIOs differ in their propensity to being subject to member state contestations in the form of exit threats and why some states are more prone to resort to threats to withdraw than others, this book utilizes Easton's systems theory as an analytical lens. It further enables the development of hypotheses on organizational and state factors, which reduce the prevalence of exits, by influencing specific and diffuse support towards the RIO in question. The empirical analysis of the hypotheses provides several important empirical insights.

First, the variation of the prevalence of exit threats between and within RIOs is not due to a single, monocausal driving force, but based on different features, most of which are linked to specific support and only one to diffuse support. Both types of support can function as buffers, preventing states from articulating discontent through withdrawal threats. Attributions of specific and diffuse support cannot prevent individual instances of dissatisfaction from occurring, but they prevent severe public contestation through threats to withdraw, which would damage the organization. In other words, by reducing the likelihood of exit threats, especially specific and, to a lesser extent, diffuse support are important for the resilience of RIOs. In other words, specific and, to a more limited extent, diffuse support play essential roles.

Second, specific support is generated when a state can ensure that its central demands are generally heard, which is the case when its inputs are overall reflected in the political system's outputs. States whose individual chances to exert general influence during the throughput stage are limited due to country features (ideological dissimilarity, limited power) and RIO institutional design features (broad policy scope, majority voting), are more likely to voice exit threats. When the state in question is significantly different from fellow member states, it is less likely to leave its imprint on RIO policies and activities in general, which reduces specific support and increases the likelihood that a specific grievance is expressed in the form of a withdrawal threat. More powerful states can translate their demands in IO outputs in most cases and this shaping ability creates a buffer of satisfaction. Hence, when the powerful state fails to make its voice heard and to exert influence concerning a specific issue, it is less likely to respond to its grievance with an exit threat. The broader the RIOs' policy mandate, the higher the number of policies and activities states can fail to exert influence on, which also increases the chances for exit threats. In addition, when an organization allows for majority voting, outvoting on contentious issues is possible. Thus, increased pooling, while having advantages in fostering smooth decision-making (Blake and Payton 2015, Hooghe and Marks 2015, Hooghe et al 2017), comes with strings attached. Such supranational features are likely to create winners and losers among the member states, reducing specific support and increasing the likelihood of threats to withdraw.

Third, next to specific support, diffuse support also reduces the propensity of exit threats, but to a more limited extent. There is only one significant driving factor: democratic socialization. Governments socialized into alterations of being winners and losers feature higher levels of generalized normative commitment to RIOs and are therefore less inclined to react to failures of exerting individual influence with threats to withdraw than their autocratic counterparts. By contrast, longer membership duration and older organizations are not prone to foster socialization and stronger ideational commitment to the organization in question, reducing the chances that states act upon a grievance with resorting to exit threats. The same applies to the democratic nature of RIOs, which is also not a significant driver of diffuse support in RIOs preventing exit threats from being voiced.

In other words, using Easton's systems theory as an analytical lens allows identifying factors behind the observed variation in exit threats between states and RIOs. States are increasingly likely to utilize withdrawal threats if they attribute limited specific and diffuse support to a particular RIO. This is the case when they cannot generally translate their demands into outputs as ideological dissimilarity, limited power, majority voting, and broad policy scopes prevent them from exerting influence in the RIO throughput process and when they are not democratically socialized. In contrast, RIOs are increasingly likely to be subjected to exit threats if they operate based on majority rules and have broad policy scopes. This is particularly pronounced if member states are ideologically diverse, when many weak states are present, and if the extent of democratic socialization is limited among RIO members.

From talking the talk to walking the walk

Institutionalized multilateral cooperation – whether at the global or regional level – can bring about disagreement and dissent among member states, as well as attempts to contest and delegitimize these organizations. Accordingly, all types of IOs as arenas of governance beyond the nation state are well-advised to develop strategies not only on how to delimit severe internal dissent, but also on how to cope with exit threats and actual exits to avoid paralysis (Hirschmann 2021, Dijkstra et al 2024, Schmidtke and Lenz 2023), disintegration (Leruth et al 2019, Rosamond 2019), and potential death (Gray 2018, Debre and Dijkstra 2021, Eilstrup-Sangiovanni 2020, 2021, von Borzyskowski and Vabulas 2024b). This suggests an important avenue for future research. While scholarship on the resilience of regional and global IOs is currently evolving and sheds light on the role of IO bureaucracies and institutional agency for IOs' ability to withstand challenges as well as the implications of resiliency-inspired reforms (for example, Wagner and Anholt 2016, Treshchenkov 2019, Ribeiro Hoffmann 2020, Debre and Dijkstra 2021, Hirschmann 2021, Dijkstra et al 2024), we still know rather little about the determinants of organizational resilience in the wake of exit threats. Further research is therefore needed to explore which institutional, procedural, and actor-related features allow IOs to respond to severe forms of internal contestation in a manner strengthening the organization at hand. Under what conditions can different types of IOs, faced with withdrawal threats or with actual withdrawals, avoid disintegration and become potentially stronger? While Brexit and the EU have been studied in this respect (for example, Rosamond 2016, Gänzle et al 2019, Chopin and Lequesne 2021, Jurado et al 2022), we do not know under what conditions exit threats are turned into actual withdrawals, thereby even more severely endangering the IO's ability to engage in effective and legitimate governance. Likewise, we do not know under what circumstances states do not implement threats to withdraw and end their contestation of the IO without escalating to actual withdrawals. As a first step towards contributing to this important avenue for research, we discuss under what conditions states might realize their exit threats and move from 'talking the talk' to 'walking the walk'.

When looking at the 73 RIOs, about 90 percent of the 123 exit threats were not followed up by an exit, and of the 56 exits only 12 were preceded by an exit threat (Panke et al 2024, 2025a). This includes six countries with just a single threat issued before withdrawing, namely Lesotho in COMESA 1997, Mauritania in ECOWAS 1999, Tanzania in COMESA 1999, Namibia in COMESA 1997, Venezuela in ANDEAN 2006, and Colombia in UNASUR 2018. Seven countries issued multiple threats before finally withdrawing, namely Morocco in the AU's predecessor (the OAU), Mozambique in COMESA, Uzbekistan in GUAM, Georgia in CIS, the UK in the EU, Russia in the CoE, as well as Kiribati in PIF. For instance, after the OAU considered and later granted Western Sahara membership in the organization, Morocco threatened to walk out six times and finally withdrew in 1984 (Interview #36, 29/08/2024). Georgia's dissatisfaction with Russian policy in its neighborhood and in CIS led to two withdrawal threats towards the Russian-dominated organization in 2001 and 2006, before Georgia turned the threat into reality in the wake of its war with Russia in 2008 (Interview #11, 03/11/2023). Colombia quickly followed through with its threat to walk out of UNASUR in 2018, which it criticized for departing from its initial aims and being inactive in the wake of the Venezuelan crises. Colombian President Iván Duque 'announced [withdrawal] in a brief televised statement, as he followed through on his pre-election pledge to get Colombia out of the bloc, which was originally intended to foster regional integration and counter US influence when it was founded in 2008' (Thai News Service 2018). By their nature, threats to leave an organization communicate discontent and indicate that withdrawing from the RIO is a possibility should dissatisfaction continue. When discontent is no longer present, states do not need to implement their threats and can refrain from actual withdrawals. An inductive analysis of LexisNexis newspaper articles of all 123 instances of threats to withdraw from a RIO suggests that there are three reasons for states talking the talk of exit threats but not walking the walk and actually withdrawing.

First, few RIOs allow for immediate exits (ANDEAN or BSEC) or within six months of notification (South Asian Association for Regional Cooperation (SAARC) or NAFTA), while others have longer procedures in place (EU, OAS, or MERCOSUR require at least two years' notice, the Benelux Economic Union, or the Economic Community of the Great Lakes Countries three years, ICGLR four years or the Central American Common Market five years).[1] Due to time lags between the exit threat and a possible actual exit, domestic change might prevent withdrawal threats from being executed. For instance, President De Gaulle threatened to exit the EU's predecessor in 1967 due to the conflict over the UK's potential membership in the organization (Centre Virtuel 2016). After Georges Pompidou assumed the Office of President, the withdrawal threat was not reiterated, paving the way for the UK's accession (Centre Virtuel 2016). The OAS–Argentina case provides another example: US President Carter had criticized Argentina's 1976 coup d'état during the OAS' regular session of the General Assembly in 1980 (World News Digest 1980). In reaction, Argentina had voiced a threat to withdraw from the OAS should the focus on and criticism of their government continue. However, Argentina returned to democratic constitutional rule in 1983, and the exit threat was not implemented.

Second, conflicts that sparked discontent and led to threats to withdraw from a RIO can lose saliency or even end, such as disagreements over a short-lived topic. For instance, Eswatini and Zimbabwe threatened to exit from COMESA in 1997 over the misappropriation of funds by a COMESA official.[2] Following an official investigation of the case, the topic was no longer important, and both countries refrained from implementing their threats. This also suggests that symbolic or signaling effects of threats can render their execution obsolete (for a set of mainly global IOs, see von Borzyskowski and

Vabulas 2023). A case in point is the exit threat of Kiribati in PIF in 2015. Kiribati's President Anote Tong took issue with Australia's stance towards climate change and generated a broader (international) audience by linking the criticism to a withdrawal threat from PIF. Stating that changes in [PIF] membership may be necessary to reach a uniform position on climate change, he suggested that either Australia or the PIF's smaller island states, which include Kiribati and six other particularly vulnerable island states, exited from PIF (PACNEWS 2015). Once the audience was reached, talk about potential withdrawal lapsed into silence. The case of Nicaragua and the OAS is an example of a symbolic exit threat applied to communicate with a domestic audience. Nicaragua issued a threat to walk out of the OAS in 2010, following an OAS resolution in favor of Costa Rica, which called for the removal of Nicaraguan soldiers in a disputed region. By employing harsh rhetoric referring to manipulation and conspiracy by the OAS, the Nicaraguan government signaled to its domestic constituency that it did not regard the OAS resolution as justified. After this message was communicated, Nicaragua – for the time being – did not follow up on the previously voiced exit threat.

A third reason why exit threats may not be carried out could lie in how RIOs respond to such threats. Reactions to exit threats can range from indifference or even encouragement by other member states and RIO officials, to sympathetic or conciliatory rhetoric, and, in some cases, to concrete concessions such as policy changes or institutional reforms.

Disregard was evident in case of the Georgian threat to exit from CIS in 2001. Responding to this threat, Russian 'President Putin on 12 October said that "the withdrawal of Georgia [from CIS] would only reduce the burden which Russia has taken on itself in view of the special relations with the republic in the political sphere," Russian agencies reported' (IPR 2001).

An example of a sympathetic and consoling response occurred in the EAC. In 2013, Tanzania had threatened to exit the EAC over its perception of being sidelined in the context of integration decision-making processes by Kenya, Rwanda, and Uganda (*Daily Monitor* 2013). As a direct reaction, 'Kenya […] reassured Tanzania that it will work together with her in matters pertaining to [EAC] integration and dispelled doubts that there are any moves to sideline it in the regional bloc' (BBC 2013b). Another example is the exit threat voiced by Kyrgyzstan vis-à-vis the EAEU in 2020, when the Central Asian state had questioned the efficacy of the organization amid the ongoing COVID-19 pandemic along with lingering border disputes with its fellow member Kazakhstan and its overall pace of integration (BBC 2020b). The Chairman of the Eurasian Economic Commission, the executive organ of the EAEU, subsequently voiced admiration for Kyrgyzstan's role in the organization and noted that 'the development of mutually beneficial cooperation between the Kyrgyz Republic and other member states of the EAEU on the basis of long traditions of friendship and mutual respect will serve to further strengthen the economies of our countries' (Impact Financial News 2020).

RIOs can also react to exit threats with concessions. Several scholars note that the non-implementation of exit threats might be linked to concessions from the organization in question, which can be related to adjustments of an IO's institutional design or in relation to policy questions (see von Borzyskowski and Vabulas 2023 for concessions, and Rosamond 2016, Gänzle et al 2019, Chopin and Lequesne 2021, Jurado et al 2022 for non-concessions in this respect). Additionally, as the example of PIF illustrates, RIO concessions, in this case the reinstatement of the rotation of the office of the PIF's Secretary General, can get accepted by some dissatisfied states, but not by others. In 2020 and 2021, the Marshall Islands, Micronesia, Nauru, and Palau had threatened to withdraw from PIF in protest of the violation of a gentlemen's agreement concerning the rotation of the post of the PIF Secretary General. On this matter, the 'Micronesians feel it is their turn at the top job and indeed that it was promised to them. They have in fact threatened to withdraw from the PIF if their candidate is not selected' (Newstex 2020). They remained in the organization after the reinstatement of the rotation principle as part of the concession. PIF apologized and established a compromise:

> Fiji's Prime Minister Frank Bainimarama used his inaugural speech as the new chair of the Pacific Islands Forum to offer an apology to the Micronesian members of the Pacific grouping who were angered by the way the Forum rejected their nominee for the Forum Secretary General job. 'I offer you my deepest apology,' said Bainimarama at the handover ceremony done virtually at the start of the 51st Pacific Islands Forum Leaders' retreat today. 'We could have handled it better,' he added. […] Outgoing Pacific Islands Forum chair Kausea Natano, who's Prime Minister of Tuvalu made mention of the Micronesians in his handover address, and although he gave no clue as to whether his attempts to win back the Micronesians into the Forum have had any success, he stressed 'unity and solidarity' for the Pacific regional bloc. (PACNEWS 2021)

Further:

> In February 2021, Micronesian leaders announced plans to leave the regional body after their candidate for secretary general of the forum was passed over in favour of a Polynesian candidate, despite a 'gentleman's agreement' that the top job should be shared between Polynesian, Melanesian and Micronesian candidates. The Micronesian leaders had signalled their intention to leave the forum at the end of June, but last-minute talks in Suva last month between key Pacific leaders, including some from Micronesia, were thought to have resolved the impasse. (*The Guardian* 2022a).

Kiribati also threatened to withdraw but was not satisfied by the concession and consequently withdrew from PIF in 2022 (*The Guardian* 2022b, The West Australian 2023). It rejoined the organization in 2023 after an apology ceremony had been conducted (Fry and Tarte 2025). This exemplifies how exit threats in RIOs calling for limited changes in these organizations can lead to concessions triggering institutional reforms (see also von Borzyskowski and Vabulas 2023).

As exit threats are public contestations of the RIO in question and signal internal discontent to the outside world, potentially undermining the organization in question or harming its standing, encouragement of exits or simply ignoring threats are rare responses. SADC comes close to this after Madagascar's threat to withdraw from the organization, when the 'SADC ambassador to Madagascar [...] confirmed that Madagascar's withdrawal from SADC was a real possibility, but said that according to SADC rules the country "would have to toe the SADC line for a year"' (Mail & Guardian 2011). Instead, in about 44 percent of exit threats, RIOs, in order to prevent further escalation, respond with rhetorical consolations in the form of public statements that express some form of solidarity with, sympathy for, and/or commitment to support the threatening state, but lack any activity or specific measures to follow up on this speech act.

Taken together, due to domestic change, altered issue salience as well as rhetorical consolations and actual concessions, only about 10 percent of exit threats lead to withdrawals, which further damage the RIO in question by reducing its membership size and budget as well as decreasing economies of scale (Panke et al 2024, 2025a).

Implications for IO resilience

This book holds a series of implications for research on the resilience of IOs in general, defined as the ability to channel or adapt to discontent in a manner maintaining the organizations' core.

First, contestations that are linked to exit threats challenge an IO's core as they publicly question the purpose of IO membership and the purpose of the IO as such. This book showed that states are likely to encounter a situation of dissatisfaction with an IO they are a member of, which constitutes the necessary condition for exit threats. Yet not all grievances are expressed in the form of exit threats. A high level of specific support attributed to an IO can function as a buffer, reducing the prevalence of exit threats. More specifically, states are most likely to issue exit threats as a means of contestation if their opportunities to influence the IO's throughput processes are generally limited. This suggests that IOs become more resilient the more inclusively they design their internal decision-making procedures. While recent research has already underlined the importance of throughput legitimacy factors for the public perception of IO legitimacy (Bernauer et al 2019), as well as the dangers of ignoring the demands for greater democratic legitimation (Kreuder-Sonnen and Rittberger 2023), we extend this argument. In doing so, we show that it also applies to governments' decisions to (not) voice withdrawal threats toward IOs. In this respect, outlining that influence over IOs' throughput processes represents a legitimation demand that, if left unaddressed, entails severe repercussions in terms of states' discontent with organizations, the book also contributes to research on IOs' legitimation strategies (Lenz and Schmidtke 2023, Schmidtke and Lenz 2023, Lenz and Söderbaum 2023).

Second, the impact of diffuse support on the occurrence of exit threats also holds implications. Recent research has paid particular attention to the contestation of IOs by those states that were previously considered a part of the 'core' of the LIO, including the US under the Trump administration (Daßler et al 2022, Kruck et al 2022, Heinkelmann-Wild et al 2024a). Yet, our analysis indicates that less democratic states are more likely to contest IOs by issuing threats to withdraw. As a result, while the contestation of institutions through core Western states may be especially salient, the contestation of rule-based multilateral governance is likely to occur on a much broader scale – as underlined by the larger number of exit threats in non-Western and relatively less-salient RIOs in our dataset.

Third, IOs are not immune from member state contestations, as expressing dissatisfaction with the IO policy or (in)activity in the form of exit threats occurs even in community organizations. This form of contestation jeopardizes the reputation, legitimacy and, potentially, the influence of the affected organization internally and vis-à-vis third-party actors. Hence, IOs are well advised to boost their resilience by strengthening specific and diffuse support respectively. This book suggests that strengthening the buffer of generalized support can be achieved by IOs through the admission of new member states that are ideologically similar to the states already in the IO, by preventing the policy scope of the organization from becoming ever broader and more encompassing, through decision-making rules that provide all member states with good opportunities to exert influence over IO policy outputs, or by supporting processes of democratization of member states. An increase in specific and diffuse support reduces the chances that a state encountering a situation of being dissatisfied with a particular IO at a given point in time resorts to withdrawal threats as a form of contestation. Moreover, the limited share of withdrawal threats being realized and turned into actual exits (see the previous section, 'From talking the talk to walking the walk') connects to previous findings that IOs in general are sticky institutions and rather robust. Hence, their death, which may be facilitated by the exit of member states, is relatively rare (Debre and Dijkstra 2021, 2023, Panke et al 2024).

Given these insights, fruitful avenues for future research could examine in a theory-guided, methodological sound and empirical manner how and under what conditions IOs can prevent different forms of contestations (including exit threats, but also mere criticism or even exits) in the first place. Also, under what conditions might it be better for the legitimacy and the effectiveness of an IO to adapt to the different contestations and undergo policy or organizational change while maintaining the IO's normative core? What is the role of IOs and other member states in this respect and which resilience procedures represent best practices? Finally, under what conditions are IOs better off in letting contestations of a member state escalate without adapting to the demands made?

Notes

one Introduction

1   There are different types of international organization (IO) in which three or more states cooperate on the basis of a treaty, which outlines the IOs policy mandate and decision-making rules, and which is supported by a secretariat as well as a headquarter office (Rittberger et al 2019). This includes rule-setting/standard-setting IOs and activity-centered/ operational IOs, democratic IOs and autocratic IOs, China-led IOs and US-led IOs or regional and global IOs (see further 'Types of international organizations and rationale for focusing on RIOs'). Thus, IO researchers are usually selective on which type of IOs they focus on. This book empirically studies regional IOs (RIOs) (see Chapter Two for the rationale of IO-type selection).

    RIOs are defined as forms of institutionalized cooperation between three or more states on the basis of primary law (founding treaty, treaty changes) with a headquarter office or a permanent secretariat. Unlike in global IOs, RIOs recruit their member states on the basis of geography-related criteria (Panke et al 2020). Accordingly, member states of RIOs tend to share more historical legacies and cultures than members of global IOs, have more similar socio-economic conditions, and face the same contextual challenges and opportunities, to a greater extent, than members of a global IO. RIOs are thus often considered to be community organizations characterized by common identities based on shared history, culture, language, and geographic proximity (Slocum and van Langenhove 2005, Thomas 2017, Spandler 2019). In effect, RIOs are closely connected to and constituted upon conceptions of regions as 'socially constructed, spatial ideas, which follow concepts of community and society' (Goltermann et al 2012: 4).

2   For instance, British Prime Minister Margret Thatcher articulated her discontent with the agrarian policy and overall budget regulations of the European Community (Backhouse 2002), the EU's predecessor, in 1979 through the (in)famous exclamation 'I want my money back' (Der Spiegel 2019). Yet, this dissatisfaction was not linked to a threat to withdraw from the EC.

    Recent examples of grievances include Indonesia or the Philippines being disappointed with the Association of Southeast Asian Nations (ASEAN) over failing to take a united stance towards the conflict in the

South Chinese Sea (Thai Examiner 2024), or Uruguay's displeasure with the Common Market of the South's (MERCOSUR) consensus-based decision-making hampering the country's economy, taking it 'hostage to Mercosur's immobility' (Newstex 2023). However, grievances are also evident in less prominent cases and in different regions. For example, in 2007 the Solomon Islands were displeased with the Pacific Island Forum (PIF) due to a regional stabilization mission that the country hosted, regarding it as interfering in its domestic affairs. While PIF conducted a review of the mission, the Solomon Islands expressed their discontent with this step, which they regarded as insufficient (Xinhua 2007). Similarly, in 2008 Senegal expressed its discontent with the African Union's (AU) approach of seeking 'African solutions to African problems', which they regarded as insufficient in the context of the ongoing Darfur crisis (Defence Web 2008).

3   We define dissatisfaction as a situation in which a member state perceives the RIOs' policy output – or the absence of a specific policy, politics or polity change – or the RIOs' (in)activities as diverging from their preferences. Throughout this book we also use grievances, discontent, displeasure, or disappointment synonymously with dissatisfaction. States can be displeased with the organization's outputs in the form of the substance or directionality of policies or activities as well as the absence of RO activity or policies in a given case. In this respect, dissatisfaction of member states with RIO output can relate to regulative or (re)distributive questions as well as questions of value attribution. A member state's grievance can also be linked to RIO polity features, such as the authority of the RIO and its extent of supranationality, as the Brexit case illustrates. Unlike policy and activity output, which states can influence in the day-to-day operation of the RIO, changing polity features usually requires treaty changes or amendments, which is not usually subject to day-to-day policy making in the RIO, but calls for special meetings, such as intergovernmental conferences or conferences of the parties. Furthermore, states can be dissatisfied with the activities of specific RIO member states and the (in)activity of the remaining members of the RIO as such to counteract or prevent the continuation of the criticized behavior or activity (for example, hostility of one, lack of solidarity of the others).

4   Specific support is generated when a state can generally ensure that its central demands are heard (while it can nevertheless happen that the state fails to get what it wants in a specific instance), which is the case when its inputs are often reflected in the political system's outputs. Accordingly, states whose individual chances to exert influence during the throughput stage are generally more limited due to country features

NOTES

(ideological dissimilarity, limited power) and RIO institutional design features (high policy scope, majority voting), are more likely to voice exit threats. When the state in question is strongly different from fellow member states, it is generally less likely to leave its imprint on RIO policies and activities, which in the longer run reduces specific support and increases the likelihood of exit threats. Also, the less powerful a state is, the more limited its abilities to generally turn its demands into RIO policy outputs, which over time also reduces the specific support. The broader the RIOs' policy mandate, the higher the number of policies and activities states can fail to exert influence, which also increases the chances for exit threats. In addition, when an organization allows for majority voting, outvoting on contentious issues is possible. Hence, increased pooling, while having advantages in fostering smooth decision-making, comes with strings attached. Such features are likely to create winners and losers among the member states, which can over time reduce specific support and increase the likelihood of exit threats.

5 Governments that are socialized into alternating between being winners and losers feature higher levels of generalized support to RIOs and are therefore less inclined to react to failures of exerting individual influence to address effectively grievances with exit threats than their autocratic counterparts.

two Regional International Organizations: Member State Dissatisfaction in Community Organizations

1 Throughout this book we also use discontent, displeasure, or disappointment synonymously with dissatisfaction or grievances.
2 In the 1980s, the UK government under Margaret Thatcher sought to reduce the UK's contributions to the EU's predecessor, the European Economic Community, and was eventually successful in achieving a 'Brits-discount' in terms of membership contribution (Backhouse 2002).

three Exit Threats as Severe Contestations

1 We use the terms 'exit' and 'withdraw' synonymously.
2 State withdrawals from RIOs – and the threat thereof – differ from adjacent concepts such as the suspension or expulsion of member states. While suspensions or expulsions represent sanctioning instruments issued by RIOs against their member states, exits and exit threats are initiated by the respective member state.

3   When the officials of a member state voice several exit threats concerning one RIO in the same year, this was counted as one instance of an exit threat, since our unit of analysis is state-RIO-year (see Chapter Five).
4   While the COW-IGO dataset constitutes an essential resource for the study of IOs over time, the book draws on the ROCO 2.0 dataset (Panke et al 2020) and extends the dataset to include the years 2021 and 2022 to cover 73 RIOs in Africa, the Americas, Asia, and Europe between 1945 and 2022 (see Table A.1 in the Appendix for a list of all RIOs and their acronyms). Compared to the COW-IGO v3.0 dataset, which features data on state membership in intergovernmental organizations in the period from 1815 to 2014 for a total of 534 mostly global IOs (Pevehouse et al 2020) and is a commonly used dataset for the study of IOs over time (see, for example, von Borzyskowski and Vabulas 2019b, Debre and Dijkstra 2021), the ROCO dataset employs the following criteria for inclusion: organizations that are based on a set of written legal rules (primary law) as well as headquarters or a secretariat in which at least three states cooperate with one another on the basis of geographic criteria in more than one narrowly defined issue area (Panke et al 2020: 1).
5   For example, in 2018 Colombia announced its '"irreversible withdrawal" from the Union of South American Nations (UNASUR)' (CENF 2018).
6   For example, Uruguay issued an exit threat to Mercosur in 2007: '[President] Vazquez has made no secret of his desire to conclude a free-trade agreement with the US, which imports more Uruguayan goods than either Argentina or Brazil. Vazquez has periodically threatened the country's withdrawal from Mercosur if steps are not taken to address trade asymmetries within the bloc or amend rules barring the pursuit of bilateral trade agreements by individual member states' (The PRS Group 2007).
7   Prominent exceptions include the League of Arab States and the Gulf Cooperation Council, which have Arabic as the sole official language but are at least partially alleviated by the presence of prominent English-language newspapers in several member states across the Middle East.
8   Thus, for example, we did not code as an exit threat the 2013 'statement by Opposition Leader Gaston Browne that he would withdraw Antigua and Barbuda from the nine-member Organisation of Eastern Caribbean States (OECS) if the headquarters of the regional airline […] moved from the island' (CANA News 2013).
9   Hence, the following statement of Venezuela in 2012 in which it threatened 'to withdraw from the Organization of American States' Inter-American Commission on Human Rights' (CNN 2012) was not coded as an exit threat.
10 We thus did not code an exit threat when 'Namibia announced it will withdraw its membership from the Common Market for Eastern and

Southern Africa (COMESA). The country announced that it would terminate its membership by the end of May next year' (BBC 2003).

four A Systems Theory Perspective on the Prevalence of Exit Threats

1. Thus, this chapter refers to IOs rather than RIOs. It ends with a reflection on similarities and differences concerning global and regional IOs and other IO types in light of the theoretical expectations developed.
2. Both 'pure' rationalist bargaining and 'pure' communicative action represent ideal types that no empirical situation will ever fully resemble (Deitelhoff and Müller 2005).
3. Distinct from pooling, IOs vary in the extent to which their member states delegate authority to IO bodies – such as secretariats and courts – as independent agents (Hooghe et al 2019b, Hooghe and Marks 2015). IOs differ specifically with regard to whether they have a court, which can adjudicate conflicts and potentially convict individual member states for rule violations. As highlighted by the legalization literature and rational institutional design approaches, courts can contribute to the solution of the free-rider problem and thus represent an incentive for states to cooperate in an organization in the first place (Abbott et al 2000). However, court rulings also reduce states' autonomy (Abbott et al 2000, Goldstein et al 2000, Kahler 2000). IO courts can potentially overrule and block states' desired policy outputs and thereby ex-post reduce their ability to shape IO outputs in line with their demands. Also, being held accountable by courts, avoiding the implementation of undesired policy outputs by the IO becomes much more difficult for states, thus de facto reducing their ability to pursue their demands. Both increase chances for exit threats. We control for this variable in the analysis (see Chapter Five).
4. This resonates with Hirschman's seminal work *Exit, Voice, and Loyalty: Responses to the Decline in Firms, Organizations, and States* (1970), which focuses on exits and not exit threats. Yet, when disregarding this difference, one could argue that Hirschman also expects exit (threats) to be more prevalent, when voice (that is, shaping a company's products or an organization's outcomes in the 'normal' participation pathways) does not work or when loyalty is absent.

five Empirical Analysis: Accounting for the Varying Prevalence of Exit Threats

1. As states are nested in RIOs, the data structure is hierarchical in nature. Therefore, we conducted a robustness check with multilevel logistic

2   regressions (see Table A.5 in the Appendix), which reveals that our findings remain robust even with a different model specification.

2   All interviews took place under conditions of anonymity; hence names, positions, and affiliation of the interview partners are not revealed in this book.

3   An example for the latter is the exit threat of Azerbaijan in the CoE in 2017. A newspaper cited a CoE member when reporting that '[r]esponding to this defiance, in October 2017 the Committee of Ministers voted to trigger legal proceedings against Azerbaijan. This means, if [imprisoned journalist Novruzali] Mammadov is not released, the European Court [of Human Rights] will be asked to further deliberate on his detention and its judgement in case no.1, and ultimately could result in a challenge to Azerbaijan's membership of the Council of Europe. President [Ilham] Aliyev has indirectly threatened to withdraw Azerbaijan from the Council of Europe, and has predictably tried to blame the current crisis on [CoE Secretary-General Thorbjorn] Jagland, when of course it is the government's obstinance that has got us to where we are today' (SNS 2017).

4   For example, Tanzania's threat to withdraw from COMESA in favor of SADC in 1999 shows that the presence of a global power within a RIO can influences states' stance towards the organization. Being confronted with the decision to withdraw from either of the organizations due to institutional overlaps, Tanzania's decision to exit COMESA while remaining in SADC is linked to the presence of G20 member South Africa in the latter. This is evident in statements made by the Tanzanian government that, by leaving COMESA, it lost only insignificant trade links (Africa News 2000c), whereas South Africa is Tanzania's largest trading partner and biggest investor (ION 2000). Similarly, commentators noted that COMESA consisted mainly of unstable states with agricultural economies, whereas South Africa represented an industrial powerhouse (The Nation 2000). Thus, Tanzania expected concrete benefits from a closer affiliation with South Africa, including the connection to the SADC electricity networks as a response to its energy crisis (Africa News 2000b), cooperation efforts within SADC to procure AIDS drugs (Africa News 2000a), as well as economic benefits from a prospective preferential trade agreement between South Africa and the EU (Muntschick 2018). Consequently, the benefits expected by Tanzania represent the sheltering effects resulting from a closer alignment with a global power.

5   This is, for example, evident in Armenia's approach toward CIS, where it pursued a 'policy of freezing the relations without an official pledge to leave the organizations because the latter would provoke a reaction from Russia' (Interview #8, 02/11/2023).

Conclusions

[1] The data on the timing entailed in withdrawal clauses has been collected on the basis of RIO primary law sources by the authors (see Chapter Five).

[2] 'The survival of COMESA, the Common Market for Eastern and Southern Africa, has come into question following allegations of financial mismanagement and power abuse against the chief executive, Dr. Bingu wa Mutharika, a Malawian national. Mutharika, who was based at the COMESA secretariat in the Zambian capital, Lusaka, was sent on forced leave in January and investigations are underway into allegations that he used official funds to finance personal political interests' (IPS 1997). Additionally, 'Mozambique, another sceptic from the outset, pulled out of COMESA early this month and a few more SADC members, including Swaziland, Namibia, Lesotho and Zimbabwe, have reportedly threatened to withdraw, but are waiting for the results on the investigations regarding Mutharika's activities are made public' (IPS 1997).

Appendix

Table A.1: List of RIOs

Abbreviation	Full name	Start	End
AC	Arctic Council	1996	
ACC	Arab Cooperation Council	1989	1990
ACD	Asia Cooperation Dialogue	2001	
ACS	Association of Caribbean States	1994	
ACTO	Amazonian Cooperation Treaty Organization	1995	
ALADI	Latin American Integration Association	1960	
ALBA	Bolivarian Alliance for the Peoples of Our Americas	2004	
AMU	Arab Maghreb Union	1989	
ANDEAN	Andean Community	1969	
APEC	Asia-Pacific Economic Cooperation	1989	
ASEAN	Association of Southeast Asian Nations	1967	
AU	African Union	1963	
BEU	Benelux Economic Union	1958	
BIMSTEC	Bay of Bengal Initiative for Multi-Sectoral Technical and Economic Cooperation	1997	
BSEC	Black Sea Economic Cooperation	1992	
CACM	Central American Common Market	1960	
CAEU	Council of Arab Economic Unity	1964	

APPENDIX

Abbreviation	Full name	Start	End
CAREC	Central Asia Regional Economic Cooperation	1997	
CARICOM	Caribbean Community	1965	
CCTS	Cooperation Council of Turkic Speaking States	2009	
CE	Conseil de l'Entente	1959	
CEEAC	Communauté Economique des États de l'Afrique Centrale	1983	
CEFTA	Central European Free Trade Agreement	1992	
CEI	Central European Initiative	1989	
CELAC	Community of Latin American and Caribbean States	2011	
CEMAC	Communauté économique et monétaire de l'Afrique centrale	1991	
CENSAD	Community of Sahel-Saharan States	1998	
CEPGL	Economic Community of the Great Lakes Countries	1976	
CICA	Conference on Interaction and Confidence Building Measures in Asia	1999	
CIS	Commonwealth of Independent States	1991	
CoE	Council of Europe	1949	
COMESA	Common Market for Eastern and Southern Africa	1993	
CSTO	Collective Security Treaty (Organization)	1992	
EAC	East African Community	1967	1977
		1999	
EAEU	Eurasian Economic Union	2000	

EXIT THREATS IN REGIONAL INTERNATIONAL ORGANIZATIONS

Abbreviation	Full name	Start	End
ECO	Economic Cooperation Organization	1985	
ECOWAS	Economic Community of West African States	1975	
EFTA	European Free Trade Association	1960	
EU	European Union	1951	
G5S	G5 Sahel	2014	
GCC	Gulf Cooperation Council	1981	
GGC	Gulf of Guinea Commission	2001	
GUAM	Organization for Democracy and Economic Development	1997	
ICGLR	International Conference on the Great Lakes Region	2004	
IGAD	Intergovernmental Authority on Development	1986	
IOC	Indian Ocean Commission	1984	
IORA	Indian Ocean Rim Association	1997	
LAS	League of Arab States	1945	
LCBC	Lake Chad Basin Commission	1964	
MERCOSUR	Mercado Comun del Sur	1994	
MGC	Mekong-Ganga Cooperation	2000	
MRU	Mano River Union	1973	
MSG	Melanesian Spearhead Group	2007	
NAFTA	North American Free Trade Organization	1994	
NATO	North Atlantic Treaty Organization	1949	
NC	Nordic Council	1952	
OAS	Organization of American States	1948	
ODECA	Organization of Central American States	1951	1973

APPENDIX

Abbreviation	Full name	Start	End
OECS	Organisation of Eastern Caribbean States	1981	
OSCE	Organisation for Security and Co-operation in Europe	1975	
PIF	Pacific Islands Forum	1971	
SAARC	South Asian Association for Regional Cooperation	1985	
SACU	Southern African Customs Union	1945	
SADC	Southern African Development Community	1980	
SCO	Shanghai Cooperation Organization	2001	
SEATO	Southeast Asia Treaty Organization	1955	1977
SELA	Latin American Economic System	1975	
SICA	Central American Integration System	1991	
SPC	Pacific Community	1947	
UEMOA	West African Economic and Monetary Union	1994	
UNASUR	Union of South American Nations	2008	
WEU	Western European Union	1955	2010
WTO	Warsaw Treaty Organisation	1955	1991

Table A.2: Newspaper coverage of RIOs

Abbr.	Full name	Approx. # of articles	First report in LexisNexis	Year established
AC	Arctic Council	<1000	1998	1996
ACC	Arab Cooperation Council	<1000	1981	1989
ACD	Asia Cooperation Dialogue	<10000	1995	2001
ACS	Association of Caribbean States	<10000	1992	1994
ACTO	Amazonian Cooperation Treaty Organization	<1000	1992	1995
ALADI	Latin American Integration Association	<10000	1980	1960
ALBA	Bolivarian Alliance for the Peoples of Our Americas	<1000	2009	2004
AMU	Arab Maghreb Union	<10000	1987	1989
ANDEAN	Andean Community	<10000	1982	1969
APEC	Asia-Pacific Economic Cooperation	<1000000	1985	1989
ASEAN	Association of Southeast Asian Nations	<1000000	1972	1967
AU	African Union	<1000000	1967	1963
BEU	Benelux Economic Union	<1000	1981	1958
BIMSTEC	Bay of Bengal Initiative for Multi-Sectoral Technical and Economic Cooperation	<10000	2004	1997
BSEC	Black Sea Economic Cooperation	<10000	1990	1992

APPENDIX

Abbr.	Full name	Approx. # of articles	First report in LexisNexis	Year established
CACM	Central American Common Market	<10000	1961	1960
CAEU	Council of Arab Economic Unity	<1000	1977	1964
CAREC	Central Asia Regional Economic Cooperation	<10000	2002	1997
CARICOM	Caribbean Community	<100000	1977	1965
CCTS	Cooperation Council of Turkic Speaking States	<10000	2009	2009
CE	Conseil de l'Entente	<10000	1982	1959
CEEAC	Communauté Economique des États de l'Afrique Centrale	<10000	1991	1983
CEFTA	Central European Free Trade Agreement	<10000	1992	1992
CEI	Central European Initiative	<10000	1991	1989
CELAC	Community of Latin American and Caribbean States	<100000	1990	2011
CEMAC	Communauté économique et monétaire de l'Afrique centrale	<10000	1994	1991
CENSAD	Community of Sahel-Saharan States	<10000	1998	1998
CEPGL	Economic Community of the Great Lakes Countries	<1000	1977	1976

Abbr.	Full name	Approx. # of articles	First report in LexisNexis	Year established
CICA	Conference on Interaction and Confidence Building Measures in Asia	<10000	1996	1999
CIS	Commonwealth of Independent States	<1000000	1989	1991
CoE	Council of Europe	<1000000	1949	1949
COMESA	Common Market for Eastern and Southern Africa	<100000	1985	1993
CSTO	Collective Security Treaty (Organization)	<100000	2001	1992
EAC	East African Community	<100000	1970	1967
				1999
EAEU	Eurasian Economic Union	<100000	1994	2000
ECO	Economic Cooperation Organization	<100000	1978	1985
ECOWAS	Economic Community of West African States	<100000	1975	1975
EFTA	European Free Trade Association	<100000	1975	1960
EU	European Union	<10000000	1948	1951
G5S	G5 Sahel	<100000	2014	2014
GCC	Gulf Cooperation Council	<1000000	1981	1981
GGC	Gulf of Guinea Commission	<10000	1990	2001
GUAM	Organization for Democracy and Economic Development	<10000	2006	1997

APPENDIX

Abbr.	Full name	Approx. # of articles	First report in LexisNexis	Year established
ICGLR	International Conference on the Great Lakes Region	<10000	1996	2004
IGAD	Intergovernmental Authority on Development	<100000	1996	1986
IOC	Indian Ocean Commission	<10000	1982	1984
IORA	Indian Ocean Rim Association	<10000	1996	1997
LAS	League of Arab States	<100000	1976	1945
LCBC	Lake Chad Basin Commission	<10000	1977	1964
MERCOSUR	Mercado Comun del Sur	<100000	1990	1994
MGC	Mekong-Ganga Cooperation	<1000	2000	2000
MRU	Mano River Union	<10000	1977	1973
MSG	Melanesian Spearhead Group	<10000	1987	2007
NAFTA	North American Free Trade Organization	<1000	1995	1994
NATO	North Atlantic Treaty Organization	<1000000	1949	1949
NC	Nordic Council	<10000	1976	1952
OAS	Organization of American States	<1000000	1951	1948
ODECA	Organization of Central American States	<1000	1991	1951
OECS	Organisation of Eastern Caribbean States	<10000	1983	1981

Abbr.	Full name	Approx. # of articles	First report in LexisNexis	Year established
OSCE	Organisation for Security and Co-operation in Europe	<100000	1994	1975
PIF	Pacific Islands Forum	<100000	1986	1971
SAARC	South Asian Association for Regional Cooperation	<100000	1985	1985
SACU	Southern African Customs Union	<10000	1980	1945
SADC	Southern African Development Community	<100000	1970	1980
SCO	Shanghai Cooperation Organization	<100000	2001	2001
SEATO	Southeast Asia Treaty Organization	<1000	1960	1955
SELA	Latin American Economic System	<10000	1975	1975
SICA	Central American Integration System	<10000	1992	1991
SPC	Pacific Community	<100000	1979	1947
UEMOA	West African Economic and Monetary Union	<10000	1994	1994
UNASUR	Union of South American Nations	<10000	2001	2008
WEU	Western European Union	<100000	1948	1955
WTO	Warsaw Treaty Organisation	<1000	1979	1955

APPENDIX

Table A.3: Summary statistics

Variable	Obs	Mean	Std. dev.	Min	Max
Exit threat	34.683	0.0035464	0.0594469	0	1
Relative state power	30.996	3.93E+08	1.23E+12	−2.07E+13	6.92E+12
Relative ideological dissimilarity of state	28.715	1512701	1378684	0	8132333
RIO majority rule	33.482	0.5266113	0.4992988	0	1
RIO policy scope	32.896	39.64306	34.26427	2	148
Socialization into cooperation	29.975	6.298331	3.270371	0	10
Socialization into RIO	32.670	21.17637	16.48965	0	75
RIO age	33.476	29.34425	2.11099	1	114
RIO democracy	29.778	6.314962	2.556858	0.878	10
RIO withdrawal clause	33.450	0.6579073	0.4744175	0	1
RIO size	33.464	21.37449	1.52599	1	56
RIO court	33.460	0.30526	0.4605243	0	1
Previous exits	33.443	0.0191669	0.1371136	0	1
Interstate conflicts	33.249	0.0061656	0.0782801	0	1
Regional hegemon	33.438	0.7211855	0.4484228	0	1
Regime complexity	34.639	4104362	1916661	0	11
RIO security competencies	33.450	5.844454	6.780927	0	24
RIO economic competencies	33.450	8.534499	6.720862	0	28

Table A.4: Correlation matrix (continues across)

Variable								
Exit threat	1							
Relative state power	−0.0194	1						
Relative ideological dissimilarity of state	0.0188	−0.0063	1					
RIO majority rule	0.0272	0.0021	−0.0824	1				
RIO policy scope	0.0418	−0.0023	0.0974	−0.0699	1			
Socialization into cooperation	−0.0268	−0.0368	−0.2320	−0.0693	0.0725	1		
Socialization into RIO	−0.0033	−0.1038	−0.1419	0.3083	0.0098	0.1613	1	
RIO age	−0.0034	0.0015	−0.1472	0.3726	0.0082	0.1764	0.7082	1
RIO democracy	−0.0115	0.0004	−0.1695	−0.0821	0.0849	0.7830	0.1802	0.2348
RIO withdrawal clause	0.0051	0.0025	−0.1605	0.3577	−0.1578	0.0790	0.2930	0.3598
RIO size	−0.0055	0.0001	0.1535	0.1868	0.1803	0.0782	0.1914	0.2482
RIO court	0.0198	0.0014	−0.0644	0.3346	0.2394	0.1009	0.2267	0.2472
Previous exits	−0.0054	0.0003	0.0118	0.0482	0.0714	−0.0009	−0.0612	−0.0552
Interstate conflicts	0.0090	−0.0263	0.0393	−0.0242	−0.0184	−0.0373	−0.0256	−0.0402
Regional hegemon	−0.0174	−0.0012	0.0837	−0.0800	−0.0466	0.2187	0.1419	0.2714
Regime complexity	0.0111	−0.0945	−0.0477	−0.1528	0.1276	0.1088	0.1330	0.0270
RIO security competencies	0.0129	−0.0006	0.0873	−0.1494	0.6974	0.0516	0.1154	0.1886
RIO economic competencies	0.0447	−0.0016	0.0160	0.0116	0.7950	0.0837	0.0121	−0.0353

APPENDIX

Variable									
1									
0.1107	1								
0.0953	−0.2345	1							
0.1325	0.3563	0.1177	1						
−0.0003	0.0820	−0.0839	0.0495	1					
−0.0649	−0.0262	−0.0048	−0.0279	0.0065	1				
0.2804	−0.0307	0.2983	−0.1331	−0.1334	0.0049	1			
0.1816	0.0272	−0.0484	0.0468	0.0245	−0.0123	0.0890	1		
0.0609	−0.1384	0.4008	0.0578	−0.0440	−0.0011	0.2229	0.1643	1	
0.1022	0.0078	−0.1469	0.2783	0.0816	−0.0356	−0.2270	0.0152	0.3276	1

Table A.5: Robustness check multilevel regressions

	Model 1	Model 2	Model 3	Model 4
Specific support				
Relative state power	−0.000**** (0.000)	−0.000**** (0.000)	−0.000**** (0.000)	−0.000**** (0.000)
Relative ideological dissimilarity of state	0.179** (0.075)	0.258**** (0.068)	0.185** (0.075)	0.267**** (0.068)
RIO majority rule	1.790*** (0.581)	1.887*** (0.601)	1.825*** (0.597)	1.957*** (0.630)
RIO policy scope	0.027**** (0.007)	0.027**** (0.007)	0.027**** (0.007)	0.028**** (0.007)
Diffuse support				
Socialization into cooperation	−0.147**** (0.044)		−0.147**** (0.044)	
Socialization into RIO	−0.011 (0.008)	−0.013 (0.008)		
RIO age			−0.012 (0.011)	−0.015 (0.011)
RIO democracy		0.036 (0.105)		0.048 (0.110)
Controls				
RIO withdrawal clause	−0.038 (0.420)	−0.086 (0.424)	−0.010 (0.428)	−0.043 (0.432)
RIO size	−0.006 (0.019)	−0.005 (0.019)	0.001 (0.021)	0.004 (0.021)
RIO court	−0.298 (0.450)	−0.511 (0.477)	−0.311 (0.452)	−0.542 (0.482)
Previous exits	−2.085** (1.050)	−2.097** (1.049)	−2.090** (1.050)	−2.111** (1.049)

APPENDIX

	Model 1	Model 2	Model 3	Model 4
Interstate conflicts	1.430* (0.759)	1.613** (0.761)	1.442* (0.759)	1.621** (0.761)
Regional hegemon	−0.887* (0.476)	−1.094** (0.494)	−0.890* (0.483)	−1.102** (0.504)
Regime complexity	0.079 (0.065)	0.098 (0.067)	0.079 (0.066)	0.099 (0.069)
var(_cons[RO_code])	2.949** (1.242)	3.004** (1.295)	3.105** (1.332)	3.266** (1.452)
Constant	−7.772**** (0.751)	−8.853**** (0.951)	−7.869**** (0.787)	−9.073**** (1.038)
Observations	27826	27826	27826	27826
AIC	1288.261	1300.639	1289.026	1301.427

Note: Standard errors in parentheses with *$p<0.1$, ** $p<0.05$, *** $p<0.01$, **** $p<0.001$

Table A.6: Robustness check with security and economic competencies

	Model 1	Model 2	Model 3	Model 4	Model 5	Model 6	Model 7	Model 8
Specific support								
Relative state power	−0.000**** (0.000)	−0.000*** (0.000)	−0.000*** (0.000)	−0.000*** (0.000)	−0.000*** (0.000)	−0.000*** (0.000)	−0.000*** (0.000)	−0.000** (0.000)
Relative ideological dissimilarity of state	0.215*** (0.073)	0.257*** (0.082)	0.216*** (0.079)	0.258*** (0.090)	0.157** (0.080)	0.222*** (0.086)	0.165* (0.084)	0.230** (0.091)
RIO majority rule	1.358**** (0.318)	1.369**** (0.313)	1.389**** (0.336)	1.409**** (0.329)	1.165**** (0.318)	1.189**** (0.324)	1.122**** (0.314)	1.155**** (0.325)
RIO policy scope (security)	0.052** (0.023)	0.052** (0.023)	0.056** (0.025)	0.057** (0.024)				
RIO policy scope (economy)					0.101**** (0.027)	0.098**** (0.027)	0.100**** (0.027)	0.097**** (0.027)
Diffuse support								
Socialization into cooperation	−0.103** (0.042)		−0.104** (0.042)		−0.129**** (0.039)		−0.130**** (0.040)	
Socialization into RIO	−0.012 (0.009)	−0.012 (0.009)			−0.013 (0.009)	−0.013 (0.009)		
RIO age			−0.008 (0.009)	−0.009 (0.009)			−0.005 (0.010)	−0.006 (0.011)
RIO democracy		−0.025 (0.070)		−0.022 (0.071)		−0.079 (0.067)		−0.080 (0.069)
With controls (omitted)								
Constant	−6.004**** (0.655)	−6.433**** (0.820)	−6.022**** (0.684)	−6.465**** (0.861)	−7.025**** (0.732)	−7.358**** (0.879)	−7.035**** (0.738)	−7.371**** (0.889)
Observations	28231	28231	28231	28231	28231	28231	28231	28231
AIC	1402.12	1412.99	1402.99	1413.88	1372.10	1385.50	1374.68	1388.25

Note: Clustered standard errors in parentheses with *$p<0.1$, **$p<0.05$, ***$p<0.01$, ****$p<0.001$

References

Abbott, Kenneth W., Robert O. Keohane, Andrew Moravcsik, Anne Marie Slaughter, and Duncan Snidal. 2000. 'The Concept of Legalization.' *International Organization* 54: 401–19.

Acharya, Amitav, and Alastair I. Johnston, eds. 2007. *Crafting Cooperation. Regional International Institutions in Comparative Perspective*. Cambridge: Cambridge University Press.

Adler, Emanuel. 2019. *World Ordering: A Social Theory of Cognitive Evolution*. Cambridge: Cambridge University Press.

Adler-Nissen, Rebecca. 2014. *Opting out of the European Union: Diplomacy, Sovereignty and European Integration*. Cambridge: Cambridge University Press.

Adler-Nissen, Rebecca, and Vincent Pouliot. 2014. 'Power in Practice: Negotiating the International Intervention in Libya.' *European Journal of International Relations* 20: 889–911.

Adler-Nissen, Rebecca, and Ayşe Zarakol. 2021. 'Struggles for Recognition: The Liberal International Order and the Merger of Its Discontents.' *International Organization* 75: 611–34.

AFP. 1999. 'Urgent – Mauritania to Quit ECOWAS Regional Grouping.' *Agence France Presse*. https://advance.lexis.com/api/document?collection=news&id=urn%3acontentItem%3a3Y6F-N4R0-00GS-K42C-00000-00&context=1516831&identityprofileid=9RZTVZ58010 [last accessed 9 October 2024].

AFP. 2007. 'Venezuela to Quit IMF, World Bank.' *Agence France Press*, 01/05/2007.

AFP. 2013. 'Without EU Reform, Risk of British Exit: Cameron.' *Agence France Press*, 23/01/2013.

AFP. 2021. 'Myanmar in Spotlight at Summit, with Junta Chief Barred.' *Agence France Press*, 25/10/2021.

Africa News. 2000a. 'Tanzania Dependent on SADC Efforts to Import Aids Drugs.' *Africa News*, 08/11/2022.

Africa News. 2000b. 'Tanzania Eyes SADC for Power Imports.' *Africa News*, 29/11/2000.

Africa News. 2000c. 'Tanzania Reaffirms Decision to Quit COMESA.' *Africa News*, 16/08/2000.

Agbo, Uchechukwu J., Nsemba E. Lenshie, and Raji R. Boye. 2018. 'West Africa from Peacekeeping to Peace Enforcement: ECOWAS and the Regulations of Regional Security.' *Conflict Studies Quarterly* 22: 18–35.

Agné, Hans, Lisa Maria Dellmuth, and Jonas Tallberg. 2015. 'Does Stakeholder Involvement Foster Democratic Legitimacy in International Organizations? An Empirical Assessment of a Normative Theory.' *The Review of International Organizations* 10: 465–88.

Ailincai, Anca. 2024. 'The Parliamentary Assembly of the Council of Europe Is at It Agaian: On the Non-Ratification of the Credetentials of Azerbaijan's Parliamnetary Delegation.' *Strasbourg Observers*, 08/03/2025.

Alderson, Kai. 2001. 'Making Sense of State Socialization.' *Review of International Studies* 27: 415–33.

Alley, Roderic. 2010. 'Fiji under Bainimarama: Brave New World or Hostage to Perdition?'. *The Journal of Pacific History* 45: 145–53.

Alter, Karen. 2014. *New Terrain of International Law: Courts, Politics, Rights*. Princeton: Princeton University Press.

Alter, Karen. 2022. 'The Promise and Perils of Theorizing International Regime Complexity in an Evolving World.' *The Review of International Organizations* 17: 375–96.

Anadolu Agency. 2024. 'Azerbaijani President Says Baku May Consider Withdrawal from Council of Europe.' *Anadolu Agency*, 28/02/2024.

API. 2006. 'Peru's President Asks Venezuela, Bolivia to Consider Withdrawal from Trade Bloc.' *Associated Press International*, 05/05/2006.

Arbatov, Alexey, and Andrei Kolesnikov. 2015. 'Does Russia Need the Council of Europe?'. *Carnegie Endowment for International Peace*. https://carnegieendowment.org/posts/2015/02/does-russia-need-the-council-of-europe?lang=en. 2025.

ARMINFO. 2015. 'Stratfor: Perspectives of Armenia and Belarus in EAEU Depend on Results of Russia–West Confrontation.' *ARMINFO News Agency*, 03/02/2015.

REFERENCES

Asia Times. 2021. 'Do or Die Moment for ASEAN in Myanmar.' *Asia Times English*, 23/04/2021.

Associated Press. 1982a. 'Efforts to Expel Turkey Blunted, but Ankara May Leave Anyway.' *Associated Press*. https://advance.lexis.com/document/?pdmfid=1516831&crid=a476becf-6c5b-4d5f-87d4-7488cd737272&pddocfullpath=%2Fshared%2Fdocument%2Fnews%2Furn%3AcontentItem%3A3SJ4-JPK0-0011-50HN-00000-00&pdcontentcomponentid=304478&pdteaserkey=sr0&pditab=allpods&ecomp=h6yyk&earg=sr0&prid=cf7e4df5-90d0-4bb9-9b7a-bff9e9756531 [last accessed 27 October 2024].

Associated Press. 1982b. 'Evren Threatens Withdrawal from Council of Europe.' *Associated Press*. https://advance.lexis.com/api/document?collection=news&id=urn:contentItem:3SJ4-JNM0-0011-54P5-00000-00&context=1516831 [last accessed 27 October 2024].

Associated Press. 2017. 'Venezuela Formally Notifies OAS It Will Leave Amid Protests.' *Associated Press*. https://apnews.com/general-news-b34d54fd03ff4c1cb3ebaa75eebdaa39 [last accessed 9 October 2024].

Atlantic Council. 2018. 'Trump Confirms He Threatened to Withdraw from NATO.' *Atlantic Council*, 23/08/2018.

Australian, The. 2008. 'Fijian Dictator Went Too Far: PM.' *The Australian*. https://catalogue.nla.gov.au/Record/000000/Offsite?url=https%3a%2f%2fsearch.ebscohost.com%2flogin.aspx%3fdirect%3dtrue%26site%3deds-live%26db%3dedsnbk%26AN%3d122B0CE70451C238 [last accessed 16 October 2024].

Backhouse, Roger E. 2002. 'The Macroeconomics of Margaret Thatcher.' *Journal of the History of Economic Thought* 24: 313–34.

Bäckstrand, Karin, Jan Aart Scholte, and Jonas Tallberg, eds. 2018. *Legitimacy in Global Governance: Sources, Processes, and Consequences*. Oxford: Oxford University Press.

Badache, Fanny. 2022. 'Unpacking the Bureaucratic Representation–Legitimacy Relationship in International Organizations: The Role of Elite Beliefs and Self-Legitimation Practices.' *Global Studies Quarterly* 2: 1–12.

Barnett, Michael, and Raymond Duvall. 2004. *Power in Global Governance*. Vol. 98. Cambridge: Cambridge University Press.

Barnett, Michael, and Martha Finnemore. 2004. *Rules for the World: International Organizations in Global Politics*. Cornell: Cornell University Press.

BBC. 2003. 'Namibia to Withdraw from Common Market for Eastern and Southern Africa.' *BBC Summary of World Broadcasts*, 16/05/2003.

BBC. 2013a. 'Burundi Threatens to Withdraw from Regional Body for Exclusion.' *BBC Monitoring Africa*, 07/11/2013.

BBC. 2013b. 'We Fully Support Tanzania's Stand on Regional Bloc – Kenyan Minister.' *BBC Monitoring Africa*, 15/11/2013.

BBC. 2015. 'BBC Monitoring Quotes from Armenian Press 31 Jan 15.' *BBC Worldwide Monitoring*. https://advance.lexis.com/document?crid=f0ba4944-2ecd-4b2a-9fcc-bef1f414bf1c&pddocfullpath=%2Fshared%2Fdocument%2Fnews%2Furn%3AcontentItem%3A5F6B-GGM1-DYRV-31BV-00000-00&pdsourcegroupingtype=&pdcontentcomponentid=10962&pdmfid=1516831&pdisurlapi=true [last accessed 23 September 2024].

BBC. 2017. 'Kazakhstan Defends Increased Checks on Kyrgyz Border.' *BBC Monitoring Central Asia Unit* 17/10/2017.

BBC. 2020a. 'Paper Analyses Kazakh Discontent with Russia-Led Economic Bloc.' *BBC Worldwide Monitoring*.

BBC. 2020b. 'Kyrgyz Expert Criticises Russia-Led Economic Union.' *BBC Monitoring Central Asia Unit*, 14/07/2020.

Bearce, David H., and Stacy Bondanella. 2007. 'Intergovernmental Organizations, Socialization, and Member-State Interest Convergence.' *International Organization* 61.

Bearce, David H., and Brandy J. Jolliff Scott. 2019. 'Popular Non-Support for International Organizations: How Extensive and What Does This Represent?'. *The Review of International Organizations* 14: 187–216.

Bergmann, Julian, and Patrick Müller. 2021. 'Failing Forward in the Eu's Common Security and Defense Policy: The Integration of Eu Crisis Management.' *Journal of European Public Policy* 28: 1669–87.

REFERENCES

Bernauer, Thomas, Steffen Mohrenberg, and Vally Koubi. 2019. 'Do Citizens Evaluate International Cooperation Based on Information About Procedural and Outcome Quality?'. *The Review of International Organizations* 15: 505–29.

Bexell, Magdalena, Kristina Jönsson, and Nora Stappert. 2020. 'Whose Legitimacy Beliefs Count? Targeted Audiences in Global Governance Legitimation Processes.' *Journal of International Relations and Development* 24: 483–508.

Blake, Daniel J, and Autumn Lockwood Payton. 2015. 'Balancing Design Objectives: Analyzing New Data on Voting Rules in Intergovernmental Organizations.' *The Review of International Organizations* 10: 377–402.

Börzel, Tanja A. 2022. *Why Noncompliance: The Politics of Law in the European Union*. Ithaca: Cornell University Press.

Börzel, Tanja A., and Thomas Risse, eds. 2016. *The Oxford Handbook of Comparative Regionalism*. Oxford: Oxford University Press.

Börzel, Tanja A., and Vera Van Hüllen, eds. 2015. *Governance Transfer by Regional Organizations: Patching Together a Global Script*. London: Palgrave.

Börzel, Tanja, and Michael Zürn. 2021. 'Contestations of the Liberal International Order: From Liberal Multilateralism to Postnational Liberalism.' *International Organization* 75: 282–305.

Börzel, Tanja A, Johannes Gerschewski, and Michael Zürn. 2024a. *The Liberal Script at the Beginning of the 21st Century: Conceptions, Components, and Tensions*: Oxford: Oxford University Press.

Börzel, Tanja A., Lukas Goltermann, and Kai Striebinger, eds. 2012a. *Roads to Regionalism: Genesis, Design, and Effects of Regional Organizations*. Aldershot: Ashgate.

Börzel, Tanja A., Tobias Hofmann, and Diana Panke. 2012b. 'Opinions, Referrals, and Judgments: Analyzing Longitudinal Patterns of Non-Compliance.' *Journal of European Public Policy* 19: 454–71.

Börzel, Tanja A., Tobias Hofmann, Diana Panke, and Carina Sprungk. 2010. 'Obstinate and Inefficient: Why Member States Do Not Comply with European Law.' *Comparative Political Studies* 43: 1363–90.

Börzel, Tanja, Thomas Risse, Stephanie B. Anderson, and Jean A. Garrison, eds. 2024b. *Polarization and Deep Contestations: The Liberal Script in the United States*. Oxford: Oxford University Press.

Briceño-Ruiz, José, and Andrea Ribeiro Hoffmann. 2015. 'Post-Hegemonic Regionalism, Unasur, and the Reconfiguration of Regional Cooperation in South America.' *Canadian Journal of Latin American & Caribbean Studies* 40: 48–62.

Brölmann, Catherine M., Richard Collins, Sufyan Droubi, and Ramses A. Wessel. 2018. 'Exiting International Organizations: A Brief Introduction.' *International Organizations Law Review* 15: 243–63.

Brown, Michael E., Sean M. Lynn-Jones, and Steven E. Miller, eds. 1996. *Debating the Democratic Peace*. Cambridge, MA: MIT Press.

Caballero Santos, Sergio. 2013. 'Mercosur, the Role of Ideas and a More Comprehensive Regionalism.' *Colombia Internacional* 78: 127–44.

CANA News. 2013. 'Government Criticizes Opposition Threats to Withdraw from OECS.' *CANA News*, 18/12/2013.

CE Noticias Financieras. 2019. 'Brazil Does Not Rule out Leaving Mercosur.' *CE Noticias Financieras*, 26/11/2019.

CE Noticias Financieras. 2023. 'Brazil Rejoins CELAC.' *CE Noticias Financieras*, 06/01/2023.

CEI. 'History Highlights.' *Central European Initiative*. https://www.cei.int/history.

CENF. 2018. 'Colombia Announces Unasur Retirement.' *CE Noticias Financieras English*, 10/08/2018.

Centre Virtuel. 2016. 'General De Gaulle's Second Veto.' *Centre Virtuel de la Connaissance sur l'Europe*. https://www.cvce.eu/en/obj/general_de_gaulle_s_second_veto-en-9aae82cd-d0da-4468-90dd-d1a50f905e9f.html.fr.wikipedia.org+8.

CFR. 2022. 'Myanmar's Troubled History: Coups, Military Rule, and Ethnic Conflict.' *Council on Foreign Relations*, 31/01/2022.

Checkel, Jeffery T. 2004. 'International Institutions and Socialization in Europe: Introduction and Framework.' *International Organization* 58: 801–26.

REFERENCES

Choi, Seung-Whan. 2022. 'Nationalism and Withdrawals from Intergovernmental Organizations: Connecting Theory and Data.' *The Review of International Organizations* 17: 205–15.

Chopin, Thierry, and Christian Lequesne. 2021. 'Disintegration Reversed: Brexit and the Cohesiveness of the EU27.' *Journal of Contemporary European Studies* 29: 419–31.

Christian, Ben. 2022. 'A Threat Rather Than a Resource: Why Voicing Internal Criticism Is Difficult in International Organisations.' *Journal of International Relations and Development* 25: 425–49.

Christian, Ben. 2025. 'Why International Organizations Don't Learn: Dissent Suppression as a Source of IO Dysfunction.' *International Studies Quarterly* 69: 1–13.

Clark, Richard, and Lindsay R. Dolan. 2020. 'Pleasing the Principal: U.S. Influence in World Bank Policymaking.' *American Journal of Political Science* 65: 36–51.

CNN. 2012. 'Venezuela's Chavez to Head Back to Cuba for More Cancer Treatment.' *CNN*, 30/04/2012.

Cogan, Jacob Katz. 2016. 'Certain Activities Carried out by Nicaragua in the Border Area (Costa Rica V. Nicaragua); Construction of a Road in Costa Rica Along the San Juan River (Nicaragua V. Costa Rica).' *American Journal of International Law* 110: 320–6.

Copelovitch, Mark, and Jon C.W. Pevehouse. 2019. 'International Organizations in a New Era of Populist Nationalism.' *The Review of International Organizations* 14: 169–86.

Country Watch. 2020. 'Foreign Policy Belarus.' *Country Watch Reviews*, 26/02/2020.

D & S. 2020. 'The Union State Ceases to Exist: Lukashenko Has Started the Process of Distancing Belarus from Russia – and Not Only Belarus.' *Defense and Security (Russia)*, 18/06/2020.

Dahlberg, Stefan, Aksel Sundström, Sören Holmberg, Bo Rothstein, Natalia Alvarado Pachon, and Cem Mert Dalli. 2022. 'The Quality of Government Basic Dataset, Version Jan22.' *University of Gothenburg: The Quality of Government Institute*. http://www.qog.pol.gu.se doi:10.18157/qogbasjan22.

Daily Monitor. 2013. 'Without Tanzania, Eac Members Will Become Extensions of Kenyan Economy.' *Daily Monitor*, 15/11/2013.

Daily Telegraph. 2006. 'Russia Threatens to Quit Group That Eased Cold War Tensions.' *Daily Telegraph.* https://advance.lexis.com/document/?pdmfid=1519360&crid=5f696331-d9a2-4780-a639-242164280faf&pddocfullpath=%2Fshared%2Fdocument%2Fnews%2Furn%3AcontentItem%3A4MHF-FH80-TX33-72NF-00000-00&pdcontentcomponentid=8109&pdteaserkey=sr4&pditab=allpods&ecomp=hc-yk&earg=sr4&prid=e52a8f90-7b82-40f7-bd2b-e1d5cb868986 [last accessed 14 October 2024].

Daßler, Benjamin. 2023. *The Institutional Topology of International Regime Complexes: Mapping Inter-Institutional Structures in Global Governance.* Oxford: Oxford University Press.

Daßler, Benjamin, Tim Heinkelmann-Wild, and Andreas Kruck. 2022. 'Wann Eskalieren Westliche Mächte Institutionelle Kontestation? Interne Kontrolle, Externe Effekte Und Modi Der Kontestation.' *Zeitschrift für Internationale Beziehungen* 29: 6–37.

Daßler, Benjamin, Tim Heinkelmann-Wild, and Andreas Kruck. 2024. 'How Negative Institutional Power Moderates Contestation: Explaining Dissatisfied Powers' Strategies Towards International Institutions.' *The Review of International Organizations.* https://link.springer.com/article/10.1007/s11558-024-09574-z.

Debre, Maria J. 2021. 'Clubs of Autocrats: Regional Organizations and Authoritarian Survival.' *The Review of International Organizations* 17: 485–511.

Debre, Maria J. 2025. *How Regional Organizations Sustain Authoritarian Rule: The Dictators' Club.* Oxford: Oxford University Press.

Debre, Maria Josepha, and Hylke Dijkstra. 2021. 'Institutional Design for a Post-Liberal Order: Why Some International Organizations Live Longer Than Others.' *European Journal of International Relations* 271: 311–39.

Debre, Maria Josepha, and Hylke Dijkstra. 2023. 'Are International Organizations in Decline? An Absolute and Relative Perspective on Institutional Change.' *Global Policy* 14(1): 16–30. https://doi.org/10.1111/1758-5899.13170.

Defence Web. 2008. 'Feature: Darfur and Peacekeeping in Africa.' *Defence Web*, 07/11/2008.

Deitelhoff, Nicole, and Harald Müller. 2005. 'Theoretical Paradise – Empirically Lost? Arguing with Habermas.' *Review of International Studies* 31: 167–79.

Deitelhoff, Nicole, and Lisbeth Zimmermann. 2019. 'Norms under Challenge: Unpacking the Dynamics of Norm Robustness.' *Global Security Studies* 4: 2–17.

Deitelhoff, Nicole, and Lisbeth Zimmermann. 2020. 'Things We Lost in the Fire: How Different Types of Contestation Affect the Robustness of International Norms.' *International Studies Review* 22: 51–76.

Dellmuth, Lisa Maria, and Jonas Tallberg. 2014. 'The Social Legitimacy of International Organisations: Interest Representation, Institutional Performance, and Confidence Extrapolation in the United Nations.' *Review of International Studies* 41: 451–75.

Dellmuth, Lisa Maria, and Jonas Tallberg. 2015. 'The Social Legitimacy of International Organisations: Interest Representation, Institutional Performance, and Confidence Extrapolation in the United Nations.' *Review of International Studies* 41: 451–75.

Dellmuth, Lisa Maria, and Jonas Tallberg. 2020. 'Why National and International Legitimacy Beliefs Are Linked: Social Trust as an Antecedent Factor.' *The Review of International Organizations* 15: 311–37.

Dellmuth, Lisa Maria, and Jonas Tallberg. 2023. *Legitimacy Politics: Elite Communication and Public Opinion in Global Governance*. Cambridge: Cambridge University Press.

Dellmuth, Lisa Maria, Jan Aart Scholte, and Jonas Tallberg. 2019. 'Institutional Sources of Legitimacy for International Organisations: Beyond Procedure Versus Performance.' *Review of International Studies* 45: 627–46.

Dellmuth, Lisa, Jan Aart Scholte, Jonas Tallberg, and Soetkin Verhaegen. 2022a. *Citizens, Elites, and the Legitimacy of Global Governance*. Oxford: Oxford University Press.

Dellmuth, Lisa, Jan Aart Scholte, Jonas Tallberg, and Soetkin Verhaegen. 2022b. 'The Elite–Citizen Gap in International Organization Legitimacy.' *American Political Science Review* 116: 283–300.

Der Spiegel. 2019. '"I Want My Money Back!": Die Briten in Europa.' *Der Spiegel*, 10/04/2019.

Desmidt, Sophie. 2019. 'Conflict Management and Prevention under the African Peace and Security Architecture (APSA) of the African Union.' *Africa Journal of Management* 5: 79–97.

Deutsche Welle. 2013. 'President Robert Mugabe Threatens to Pull out of SADC.' *Deutsche Welle*, 05/07/2013.

Dijkstra, Hylke, and Maria J. Debre. 2022. 'The Death of Major International Organizations: When Institutional Stickiness Is Not Enough.' *Global Studies Quarterly* 2(4): ksac048. https://doi.org/10.1093/isagsq/ksac048.

Dijkstra, Hylke, and Farsan Ghassim. 2024. 'Are Authoritative International Organizations Challenged More? A Recurrent Event Analysis of Member State Criticisms and Withdrawals.' *The Review of International Organizations*. https://doi.org/10.1007/s11558-024-09557-0.

Dingwerth, Klaus, Henning Schmidtke, and Tobias Weise. 2019a. 'The Rise of Democratic Legitimation: Why International Organizations Speak the Language of Democracy.' *European Journal of International Relations* 26: 714–41.

Dijkstra, Hylke, Laura von Allwörden, Leonard A. Schuette, and Giuseppe Zaccaria. 2024. 'Donald Trump and the Survival Strategies of International Organisations: When Can Institutional Actors Counter Existential Challenges?'. *Cambridge Review of International Affairs* 37: 182–205.

Dijkstra, Hylke, Laura von Allwörden, Leonard A. Schuette, and Giuseppe Zaccaria. 2025. *The Survival of International Organizations: Institutional Responses to Existential Challenges*. Oxford: Oxford University Press.

Dingwerth, Klaus, Antonia Witt, Ina Lehmann, Ellen Reichel, and Tobias Weise, eds. 2019b. *International Organizations under Pressure: Legitimating Global Governance in Challenging Times*. Oxford: Oxford University Press.

Drezemczewski, Andrejz. 2020. 'The (Non-) Participation of Russian Parliamentarians in the Parliamentary Assembly of the Council of Europe: An Overview of Recent Developments.' *Europe of Rights & Liberties* 1: 7–15.

Drezemczewski, Andrejz, and Kanstantsin Dzehtsiarou. 2018. 'Painful Relations between the Council of Europe and Russia.' *European Journal of International Law Talk*, 28/09/2018.

Druckman, Daniel. 1977. *Negotiations: Social–Psychological Perspectives*. Beverly Hills: Sage.

Easton, David. 1965. *A Systems Analysis of Political Life*. New York: Wiley & Sons.

Ecker-Ehrhardt, Matthias. 2012. 'Cosmopolitan Politicization: How Perceptions of Interdependence Foster Citizens' Expectations in International Institutions.' *European Journal of International Relations* 18: 481–508.

Ecker-Ehrhardt, Matthias. 2018. 'International Organizations "Going Public"? An Event History Analysis of Public Communication Reforms 1950–2015.' *International Studies Quarterly* 62: 723–36.

Ecker-Ehrhardt, Matthias, Lisa Dellmuth, and Jonas Tallberg. 2024. 'Ideology and Legitimacy in Global Governance.' *International Organization* 78: 731–65.

Eilstrup-Sangiovanni, Mette. 2020. 'Death of International Organizations: The Organizational Ecology of Intergovernmental Organizations, 1815–2015.' *The Review of International Organizations* 15: 339–70.

Eilstrup-Sangiovanni, Mette. 2021. 'What Kills International Organisations? When and Why International Organisations Terminate.' *European Journal of International Relations* 27: 281–310.

Eilstrup-Sangiovanni, Mette, and Stephanie C. Hofmann. 2020. 'Of the Contemporary Global Order, Crisis, and Change.' *Journal of European Public Policy* 27: 1077–89.

Engel, Ulf, and Frank Mattheis, eds. 2019. *The Political Economy of Regional Security Organizations*. London: Routledge.

ERR. 2019. 'Estonian Delegation Leaves Pace Session in Protest.' *ERR News*, 27/06/2019.

Eurasia Diary. 2019. 'Russia Seeks to Introduce Single Currency in Eaeu.' *Eurasia Diary*, 08/02/2019.

EVN. 2009. 'Venezuela: Country Condemns Human Rights Report, Country May Exit OAS.' *Esmerk Venezuela News*, 02/09/2009.

Ezquerro-Cañete, Arturo, and Ramón Fogel. 2017. 'A Coup Foretold: Fernando Lugo and the Lost Promise of Agrarian Reform in Paraguay.' *Journal of Agrarian Change* 17: 279–95.

Fergusson, Niall, and Fareed Zakaria. 2017. *End of the Liberal Order?*: London: Oneworld Publications.

Ferreira, Túlio S.H., and Ana C.A.C. Paiva. 2022. 'Questioning Paraguay's Suspension from Mercosur: The First Application of the Democratic Clause of the Regional Bloc.' *Contexto Internacional* 44: 1–21.

Financial Times, The. 2008. 'Leaders of Pacific Grouping Warn Fiji.' *The Financial Times*, 21/08/2008.

Fry, Greg. 2021. 'The Pacific Islands Forum Split: Possibilities for Pacific Diplomacy.' *DevPolicy Blog*. https://devpolicy.org/the-pacific-islands-forum-split-possibilities-for-pacific-diplomacy-20210223/.

Fry, Greg, and Sandra Tarte. 2025. '"New Pacific Diplomacy" Ten Years On.' *Australian Journal of International Affairs* 79: 55–63.

Fuhse, Jan. 2005. *Theorien Des Politischen Systems*. Wiesbaden: VS Verlag für Sozialwissenschaften.

Gänzle, Stefan. 2019. 'Differentiated (Dis)Integration in Europe and Beyond. Historical and Comparative Perspectives.' In *Differentiated Integration and Disintegration in a Post-Brexit Era*, eds. Stefan Gänzle, Benjamin Leruth, and Jarle Trondal. London: Routledge.

Gänzle, Stefan, Benjamin Leruth, and Jarle Trondal, eds. 2019. *Differentiated Integration and Disintegration in a Post-Brexit Era*. London: Routledge.

Gartzke, Erik. 1998. 'Kant We All Just Get Along? Opportunity, Willingness, and the Origins of the Democratic Peace.' *American Journal of Political Science* 42: 1–27.

Gast, Ann-Sophie. 2023. 'The Eurasian Economic Union: Keeping up with the EU and China.' In *Global Governance and Interaction between International Institutions: Eurasian International Organizations in the World Politics and Economy*, eds. Alexander Libman and Anastassia Obydenkova. London: Routledge.

REFERENCES

Ghebali, Victor-Yves. 2005. 'Growing Pains at the OSCE: The Rise and Fall of Russia's Pan-European Expectations.' *Cambridge Review of International Affairs* 18: 375–88.

Gleditsch, Nils Petter, Peter Wallensteen, Mikael Eriksson, Margareta Sollenberg, and Håvard Strand. 2002. 'Armed Conflict 1946–2001: A New Dataset.' *Journal of Peace Research* 39.

Goldstein, Judith, Miles Kahler, Robert O. Keohane, and Anne-Marie Slaughter. 2000. 'Legalization and World Politics.' *International Organization, Special Issue* 54.

Goltermann, Lukas, Mathis Lohaus, Alexander Spielau, and Kai Striebinger. 2012. 'Roads to Regionalism: Concepts, Issues, and Cases.' In *Roads to Regionalism. Genesis, Design and Effects of Regional Organizations*, eds. Tanja A. Börzel, Lukas Goltermann, Mathis Lohaus and Kai Striebinger. Aldershot: Ashgate. 3–21.

Gómez-Mera, Laura. 2013. *Power and Regionalism in Latin America: The Politics of Mercosur*. Notre Dame: University of Notre Dame Press.

Gray, Julia. 2018. 'Life, Death, or Zombie? The Vitality of International Organizations.' *International Studies Quarterly* 62: 1–13.

Greenhill, Brian. 2010. 'The Company You Keep: International Socialization and the Diffusion of Human Rights Norms.' *International Studies Quarterly* 54: 127–45.

Gronau, Jennifer, and Henning Schmidtke. 2015. 'The Quest for Legitimacy in World Politics – International Institutions' Legitimation Strategies.' *Review of International Studies* 42: 535–57.

Grundsfeld, Lukas. 2024. 'Cooperation or Obstruction? International Organizations and Suspensions of Member States under Regime Complexity.' Paper presented at the International Studies Association's 65th Annual Convention, San Francisco.

Guardian, The. 2016. 'Venezuelan President Is to Blame for Humanitarian Crisis, OAS Chief Says.' *The Guardian*, 24/06/2016.

Guardian, The. 2022a. 'China Influenced Kiribati Exit from Pacific Islands Forum, MP Claims.' *The Guardian*, 12/07/2021.

Guardian, The. 2022b. 'Pacific Islands Forum: Ardern Says Total Membership "Critical" as PIF Shaken by Kiribati's Exit.' *The Guardian*, 11/06/2022.

Haas, Peter M. 2016. 'Regional Environmental Governance.' In *The Oxford Handbook of Comparative Regionalism*, eds. Tanja A. Börzel and Thomas Risse. Oxford: Oxford University Press. 430–56.

Habermas, Jürgen. 1995a. *Theorie Des Kommunikativen Handelns. Band 1 Handlungsrationalität Und Gesellschaftliche Rationalisierung.* Frankfurt am Main: Suhrkamp.

Habermas, Jürgen. 1995b. *Theorie Des Kommunikativen Handelns. Band 2 Zur Kritik Der Funktionalistischen Vernunft.* Frankfurt am Main: Suhrkamp.

Haftel, Yoram, and Stephanie Hofmann. 2019. 'Rivalry and Overlap: Why Regional Economic Organizations Encroach on Security Organizations.' *Journal of Conflict Resolution* 63: 2180–206.

Haftel, Yoram, and Tobias Lenz. 2022. 'Measuring Institutional Overlap in Global Governance.' *Review of International Organizations*. https://link.springer.com/article/10.1007/s11558-021-09415-3.

Haftel, Yoram, and Bar Nadel. 2024. 'Economic Crises and the Survival of International Organizations.' *The Review of International Organizations*. https://link.springer.com/article/10.1007/s11558-024-09549-0.

Hartmann, Christof, and Kai Striebinger. 2015. 'Writing the Script? ECOWAS's Military Intervention Mechanism.' In *Governance Transfer by Regional Organizations: Patching Together a Global Script*, eds. Tanja A. Börzel and Vera Van Hüllen. London: Routledge. 68–83.

Heinkelmann-Wild, Tim, Andreas Kruck, and Bernard Zangl. 2024a. 'The Cooptation Dilemma: Explaining US Contestation of the Liberal Trade Order.' *Global Studies Quarterly* 4. https://doi.org/10.1093/isagsq/ksae024.

Heinkelmann-Wild, Tim, Berthold Rittberger, Bernard Zangl, and Lisa Kriegmair. 2024b. *European Blame Games: Where Does the Buck Stop?* Oxford: Oxford University Press.

Henning, Randall C., and Tyler Pratt. 2023. 'Hierarchy and Differentiation in International Regime Complexes: A Theoretical Framework for Comparative Research.' *Review of International Political Economy* 30: 2178–205.

REFERENCES

Herz, Monica. 2011. *The Organization of American States (OAS): Global Governance Away from the Media*. London: Routledge.

Herz, Monica, Maira Siman, and Anna Clara Telles. 2017. 'Regional Organizations, Conflict Resolution and Mediation in South America.' In *Power Dynamics and Reginal Security in Latin America*, eds. Marcial A.G. Suarez, Rafael Duarte Villa, and Brigitte Weiffen. London: Palgrave Macmillan. 123–42.

Hey, Jeanne A.K. 2003. *Small States in World Politics: Explaining Foreign Policy Behavior*. Boulder: Lynne Rienner Publishers.

Hirschman, Albert O. 1970. *Exit, Voice, and Loyalty: Responses to the Decline in Firms, Organizations, and States*. Cambridge, MA: Harvard University Press.

Hirschmann, Gisela. 2020. 'To Be or Not to Be? Lebensdynamiken Internationaler Organisationen Im Spannungsfeld Von Internationaler Autorität Und Nationalstaatlicher Souveränität.' *Zeitschrift für Internationale Beziehungen* 27: 69–93.

Hirschmann, Gisela. 2021. 'International Organizations' Responses to Member State Contestation: From Inertia to Resilience.' *International Affairs* 97: 1963–81.

Hofmann, Stephanie C. 2019. 'The Politics of Overlapping Organizations: Hostage-Taking, Forum-Shopping and Brokering.' *Journal of European Public Policy* 26: 883–905.

Hohlstein, Franziska. 2022. *Regional Organizations and Their Responses to Coups: Measures, Motives and Aims*. Bristol: Bristol University Press.

Hooghe, Liesbet, and Gary Marks. 2015. 'Delegation and Pooling in International Organizations.' *Review of International Organizations* 10: 305–28.

Hooghe, Liesbet, Tobias Lenz, and Gary Marks. 2019a. 'Contested World Order: The Delegitimation of International Governance.' *The Review of International Organizations* 14: 731–43.

Hooghe, Liesbet, Tobias Lenz, and Gary Marks. 2019b. *A Theory of International Organization*. Oxford: Oxford University Press.

Hooghe, Liesbet, Gary Marks, Tobias Lenz, Jeanine Bezuijen, Besir Ceka, and Svet Derderyan. 2017. *Measuring International Authority: A Postfunctionalist Theory of Governance*. Vol. 3. Oxford: Oxford University Press.

Houde, Anne-Marie. 2023. 'Emotions, International Relations, and the Everyday: Individuals' Emotional Attachments to International Organisations.' *Review of International Studies*: 1–19.

Ikenberry, G. John. 2018. 'The End of Liberal International Order?'. *International Affairs* 94: 7–23.

Impact Financial News. 2020. '"Mikhail Myasnikovich Congratulated Sooronbay Jeenbekov on Independence Day of the Kyrgyz Republic".' *Impact Financial News*, 01/01/2020.

Ingebritsen, Christine, Iver B. Neumann, Sieglinde Gstoehl, and Jessica Beyer, eds. 2006. *Small States in International Relations*. Seattle: University of Washington Press.

Inside Costa Rica. 2010. 'Nicaraguan Politicians Urge Ortega to Pull Troops.' *Inside Costa Rica*, 15/11/2010.

Intellinews. 2019. 'Ukrainian Delegation Suspends Its Participation in Pace.' *Intellinews*, 26/06/2019.

ION. 2000. 'Development Isn't in the Bag.' *The Indian Ocean Newsletter*, 29/01/2000.

IPR. 2001. 'Putin Reacts Calmly to Possibility That Georgia Might Quit CIS.' *IPR Strategic Business Information Database*, 16/10/2001.

IPS. 1997. 'Malawi: COMESA's Survival Threatened.' *Inter Press Service*, 07/04/1997.

Japan Times, The. 2022. 'Kiribati Withdraws from Pacific Island Forum in Blow to Regional Unity.' *The Japan Times*, 11/07/2022.

Jatobá, Daniel, and Bruno Theodoro Luciano. 2018. 'The Deposition of Paraguayan President Fernando Lugo and Its Repercussions in South American Regional Organizations.' *Brazilian Political Science Review* 12.

Johnston, Alastair Iain. 2001. 'Treating International Institutions as Social Environmentstreating International Institutions as Social Environments.' *International Studies Quarterly* 45: 487–515.

REFERENCES

Johnstone, Ian. 2003. 'Security Council Deliberations: The Power of the Better Argument.' *European Journal of International Law* 14: 437–80.

Jurado, Ignacio, Sandra León, and Stefanie Walter. 2022. 'Brexit Dilemmas: Shaping Postwithdrawal Relations with a Leaving State.' *International Organization* 76: 273–304.

Kacowicz, Arie M., and Galia Press-Barnathan. 2016. 'Regional Security Goverance.' In *Handbook of Comparative Regionalism*, eds. Tanja A. Börzel and Thomas Risse. Oxford: Oxford University Press Oxford. 297–322.

Kahler, Miles. 2000. 'Conclusion: The Causes and Consequences of Legalization.' *International Organization* 54: 661–83.

Kanté, Aïssatou, Fahiraman Rodrigue Koné, Hassane Koné, Issaka K. Souaré, and Djiby Sow. 2024. 'Rethinking Responses to Unconstitutional Changes of Government in West Africa.' Institute for Security Studies. https://issafrica.org/research/west-africa-report/rethinking-responses-to-unconstitutional-changes-of-government-in-west-africa.

Kelley, Judith. 2004. 'International Actors on the Domestic Scene: Membership Conditionality and Socialization by International Institutions.' *International Organization* 58: 425–57.

Keohane, Robert O. 1984. *After Hegemony. Cooperation and Discord in the World Political Economy*. Princeton: Princeton University Press.

Keohane, Robert O. 1989. *International Institutions and State Power*. Boulder: Westview.

Kim, Soo Yeon, Edward D. Mansfield, and Helen V. Milner. 2016. 'Regional Trade Governance.' In *Handbook of Comparative Regionalism*, eds. Tanja A. Börzel and Thomas Risse. Oxford: Oxford University Press. 323–50.

King, Gary, and Langche Zeng. 2001a. 'Explaining Rare Events in International Relations.' *International Organization* 55: 693–715.

King, Gary, and Langche Zeng. 2001b. 'Logistic Regression in Rare Events Data.' *Political Analysis* 9: 137–63.

Koremenos, Barbara, Charles Lipson, and Duncan Snidal. 2001. 'The Rational Design of International Institutions.' *International Organization* 55: 761–99.

Kreuder-Sonnen, Christian, and Berthold Rittberger. 2023. 'The Lio's Growing Democracy Gap: An Endogenous Source of Polity Contestation.' *Journal of International Relations and Development* 26: 61–85.

Kreuder-Sonnen, Christian, and Bernhard Zangl. 2016. 'Varieties of Contested Multilateralism: Positive and Negative Consequences for the Constitutionalisation of Multilateral Institutions.' *Global Constitutionalism* 5: 327–43.

Kreuder-Sonnen, Christian, and Bernhard Zangl. 2024. 'The Politics of IO Authority Transfers: Explaining Informal Internationalisation and Unilateral Renationalisation.' *Journal of European Public Policy*: 1–26.

Kruck, Andreas, Tim Heinkelmann-Wild, Benjamin Daßler, and Raphaela Hobbach. 2022. 'Disentangling Institutional Contestation by Established Powers: Types of Contestation Frames and Varying Opportunities for the Re-Legitimation of International Institutions.' *Global Constitutionalism* 11: 344–68.

Kuziemko, Ilyana, and Eric Werker. 2006. 'How Much Is a Seat on the Security Council Worth? Foreign Aid and Bribery at the United Nations.' *Journal of Political Economy* 114: 905–30.

Laffan, Brigid. 2021. 'Sovereignty and Brexit: From Theory to Practice.' *Brexit Institute Working Paper Series* 05/2021.

Laffan, Brigid, and Stefan Telle. 2023. *The EU's Response to Brexit: United and Effective*. Cham: Springer.

Lake, David A., Lisa L. Martin, and Thomas Risse. 2021. 'Challenges to the Liberal Order: Reflections on International Organization.' *International Organization* 75: 225–57.

Langlet, Arne, and Alice Vadrot. 2023. 'Negotiating Regime Complexity: Following a Regime Complex in the Making.' *Review of International Studies* 50: 231–51.

Lavenex, Sandra. 2019. 'Regional Migration Governance – Building Block of Global Initiatives?'. *Journal of Ethnic and Migration Studies* 45: 1275–93.

Lenz, Tobias. 2021. *Interorganizational Diffusion in International Relations: Regional Institutions and the Role of the European Union*. Oxford: Oxford University Press.

REFERENCES

Lenz, Tobias, and Gary Marks. 2016. 'Regional Institutional Design.' In *The Oxford Handbook of Comparative Regionalism*, eds. Tanja A. Börzel and Thomas Risse. Oxford: Oxford University Press. 513–37.

Lenz, Tobias, and Henning Schmidtke. 2023. 'Agents, Audiences and Peers: Why International Organizations Diversify Their Legitimation Discourse.' *International Affairs* 99: 921–40.

Lenz, Tobias, and Frederik Söderbaum. 2023. 'The Origins of Legitimation Strategies in International Organizations: Agents, Audiences and Environments.' *International Affairs* 99: 899–920.

Leruth, Benjamin, Stefan Gänzle, and Jarle Trondal. 2019. 'Exploring Differentiated Disintegration in a Post-Brexit European Union.' *Journal of Common Market Studies* 57: 1013–30.

Lenz, Tobias, Jeanine Bezuijen, Liesbet Hooghe, and Gary Marks. 2015. 'Patterns of International Organization: Task Specific Vs. General Purpose.' *Politische Vierteljahresschrift* 49: 107–32.

Libman, Alexander. 2011. *Commonwealth of Independent States and Eurasian Economic Community*. Moncalieri: International Democracy Watch.

Libman, Alexander. 2019. 'Learning from the European Union? Eurasian Regionalism and the "Global Script".' *Outlines of Global Transformations: Politics, Economics, Law* 12: 247–68.

Libman, Alexander, and Anastassia Obydenkova. 2020. 'Global Governance and Interaction between International Institutions: The Challenge of the Eurasian International Organizations.' *Post-Communist Economies* 33: 147–49.

Lipscy, Phillip Y. 2015. 'Explaining Institutional Change: Policy Areas, Outside Options, and the Bretton Woods Institutions.' *American Journal of Political Science* 59: 341–56.

Lipscy, Phillip Y. 2017. *Renegotiating the World Order: Institutional Change in International Relations*. Cambridge: Cambridge University Press.

Mail & Guardian. 2011. 'SADC in a Bind over Madagascar Road Map.' *Mail & Guardian*, 20/05/2011.

Mail & Guardian. 2013. 'Zimbabwe Can't Leave SADC Just Yet.' *Mail & Guardian*, 12/07/2013.

March, James G., and Johan P. Olsen. 1998. 'The Institutional Dynamics of International Political Orders.' *International Organization* 52: 943–69.

Meissner, Katharina L. 2017. 'MERCOSUR: The Ups and Downs of Regional Integration in South America.' In *Regional Integration in the Global South: External Influence on Economic Cooperation in ASEAN, MERCOSUR and SADC*, ed. Sebastian Krapohl. Cham: Springer. 147–78.

Mercopress. 2012. 'Venezuela's Mercosur Membership "Null and Void" Says Paraguayan Government.' *MercoPress*, 01/08/2012.

Milewicz, Karolina M., and Robert E. Goodin. 2016. 'Deliberative Capacity Building through International Organizations: The Case of the Universal Periodic Review of Human Rights.' *British Journal of Political Science* 48: 513–33.

Milewicz, Karolina M., and Duncan Snidal. 2016. 'Cooperation by Treaty: The Role of Multilateral Powers.' *International Organization* 70: 823–44.

Mitzen, Jennifer. 2005. 'Reading Habermas in Anarchy: Multilateral Diplomacy and Global Public Spheres.' *The American Political Science Review* 99: 401–17.

Moravcsik, Andrew. 1998. *The Choice for Europe: Social Purpose and State Power from Messina to Maastricht*. Ithaca and New York: Cornell University Press.

Mosser, Michael W. 2015. 'Embracing "Embedded Security": The OSCE's Understated but Significant Role in the European Security Architecture.' *European Security* 24: 579–99.

Müller, Daniel. 2018. 'The Saga of the 1858 Treaty of Limits: The Cases against Costa Rica.' In *Nicaragua Before the International Court of Justice: Impacts on International Law*, eds. Edgardo Sobenes Obregon and Benjamin Samson. Cham: Springer. 85–112.

Müller, Harald. 2004. 'Arguing, Bargaining and All That: Reflections on the Relationship of Communicative Action and Rationalist Theory in Analysing International Negotiations.' *European Journal of International Relations* 10: 395–435.

REFERENCES

Müller, Lukas Maximilian. 2023. *The Rise of a Regional Institution in Africa: Agency and Policy-Formation within the ECOWAS Commission.* London: Routledge.

Mumby, Jane. 2023. *Dismantling the League of Nations: The Quiet Death of an International Organization, 1945–8.* London: Bloomsbury.

Muntschick, Johannes. 2018. *The Southern African Development Community (SADC) and the European Union (EU): Regionalism and External Influence.* Basingstoke: Palgrave.

Murdoch, Zuzana, Hussein Kassim, Sara Connolly, and Benny Geys. 2018. 'Do International Institutions Matter? Socialization and International Bureaucrats.' *European Journal of International Relations* 25: 852–77.

NACLA. 2022. 'Summit of the Americas Underlines Widespread Discontent with U.S. Policy.' *North American Congress on Latin America*, 16/06/2022.

Nation, The. 2000. 'Tanzania: Dar's Decision to Quit COMESA Not Approved.' *The Nation*, 06/04/2000.

Nation, The. 2017. 'Reps Mull Nigeria Leaving ECOWAS over Morocco's Application.' *The Nation.* https://thenationonlineng.net/reps-mull-nigeria-leaving-ecowas-moroccos-application/ [last accessed 10 October 2024].

Nair, Deepak. 2019. 'Saving Face in Diplomacy: A Political Sociology of Face-to-Face Interactions in the Association of Southeast Asian Nations.' *European Journal of International Relations* 25: 672–97.

Ndlovu-Gatsheni, Sabelo. 2011. 'Reconstructing the Implications of Liberation Struggle History on SADC Mediation in Zimbabwe.' In *Secondary Reconstructing the Implications of Liberation Struggle History on SADC Mediation in Zimbabwe*, ed. Sabelo Ndlovu-Gatsheni. Johannesburg: South African Institute of International Affairs.

Newstex. 2020. 'The Pacific Islands Forum Leadership: Who and for What?'. *Newstex Blogs The Development Policy Centre Blog*, 11/11/2020.

Newstex. 2023. 'What Milei Means for Mercosur.' *Newstex Blogs The Development Policy Centre Blog*, 18/12/2023.

Nolte, Detlef, and Victor M. Mijares. 2022. 'UNASUR: An Eclectic Analytical Perspective of Its Disintegration.' *Columbia Internacional III*: 83–109.

Nolte, Detlef, and Leslie Wehner. 2013. 'UNASUR and Regional Security in South America.' In *Regional Organisations and Security*, eds. Stephen Aris and Andreas Wenger. London: Routledge. 201–20.

Nolte, Detlef, and Brigitte Weiffen, eds. 2021. *Regionalism under Stress: Europe and Latin America in Comparative Perspective*. Abingdon: Routledge.

OAS. 2010. 'OAS Secretary General Presents Recommendations Following Visit to Costa Rica and Nicaragua.' *Organization of American States*. https://www.oas.org/en/media_center/press_release.asp?sCodigo=E-425/10.

OAS. 2018. 'Proceedings Volume I, Forty-Eight Regular Session.' ed. General Assembly.

OAS. 2025. 'Organization of American States.' *Organization of American States*. https://www.oas.org/en/.

Obydenkova, Anastassia V., and Alexander Libman. 2019. *Authoritarian Regionalism in the World of International Organizations: Global Perspective and the Eurasian Enigma*. Oxford: Oxford University Press.

Olivari, Denisse R. 2014. 'The Role of the Organization of American States in Promoting FDemocracy.' *International Institute for Democracy and Electoral Assistance*. https://www.idea.int/publications/catalogue/role-organization-american-states-promoting-democracy.

Oshita, Oshita O., and Warisu O. Alli. 2021. 'Nigeria's Role in the ECOWAS Peace and Security Agenda for West Africa.' In *Regional Economic Communities and Peacebuilding in Africa: Lessons from ECOWAS and IGAD*, eds. Victor Adetula, Redie Bereketeab, and Cyril I. Obi. Milton: Taylor and Francis. 109–22.

Owen, John M. 1996. 'How Liberalism Produces Democratic Peace.' In *Debating the Democratic Peace*, eds. Michael E. Brown, Sean M. Lynn-Jones, and Steven E. Miller. Cambridge: Cambridge University Press.

REFERENCES

PACE. 2014. 'Resolution 1990: Reconsideration on Substantive Grounds of the Previously Ratified Credentials of the Russian Delegation.' ed. Parliamentary Assembly. Strasbourg: Council of Europe.

PACNEWS. 2015. 'Kiribati President Tong Warns of Split in Forum over Climate Change.' *PACNEWS*, 09/09/2015.

PACNEWS. 2021. 'We Are Sorry, Pacific Forum Chair Tells Micronesia.' *PACNEWS*, 06/08/2021.

Panafrican News Agency. 2000. 'Mauritania Quits ECOWAS Tuesday.' *Panafrican News Agency, All Africa*. https://allafrica.com/stories/200012260007.html [last accessed 9 October 2024].

Panke, Diana. 2010a. *Small States in the European Union: Coping with Structural Disadvantages*. Farnham: Ashgate.

Panke, Diana. 2010b. 'Why Big States Cannot Do What They Want. International Courts and Compliance.' *International Politics* 47: 186–209.

Panke, Diana. 2010c. 'Why Discourse Matters Only Sometimes. Effective Arguing Beyond the Nation-State.' *Review of International Studies* 36: 145–68.

Panke, Diana. 2013. *Unequal Actors in Equalising Institutions: Negotiations in the United Nations General Assembly*. Houndmills: Palgrave.

Panke, Diana. 2020. 'Regional Cooperation through the Lenses of States: Why Do States Nurture Regional Integration?'. *The Review of International Organizations* 15: 475–504.

Panke, Diana, and Sören Stapel. 2018. 'Exploring Overlapping Regionalism.' *Journal of International Relations and Development* 21: 635–62.

Panke, Diana, and Sören Stapel. 2025. *International Organizations and the Management of Regime Complexity: Disregard, Confrontation, Coordination, and Cooperation*. Oxford: Oxford University Press.

Panke, Diana, Lukas Grundsfeld, and Pawel Tverskoi. 2024. 'Between Crisis and Revival: Withdrawal Threats, State Exits, and Institutional Change of Regional International Organizations.' *Politische Vierteljahresschrift*. https://link.springer.com/article/10.1007/s11615-024-00560-z.

Panke, Diana, Lukas Grundsfeld, and Pawel Tverskoi. 2025a. 'Exit from Regime Complexity? Regional International Organizations under Scrutiny.' *Global Studies Quarterly* 5(1). https://doi.org/10.1093/isagsq/ksae078.

Panke, Diana, Lukas Grundsfeld, and Pawel Tverskoi. 2025b. 'Regional Organisations, Exit Threats, and Contestations of Community Norms.' In *Contestation in Prism – the Evolution of Norms and Norm Clusters in Contemporary Global Politics*, eds. Flavia Lucenti, Cecilia Ducci, Carmen Wunderlich, and Jeffrey S Lantis. Cham: Springer. 45–63.

Panke, Diana, Franziska Hohlstein, and Gurur Polat. 2022. 'Why International Organizations Differ in Their Output Productivity: A Comparative Study.' *International Studies Perspectives* 28: 398–424.

Panke, Diana, Stefan Lang, and Anke Wiedemann. 2018. *Regional Actors in Multilateral Negotiations: Active and Successful?* London: ECPR Press.

Panke, Diana, Gurur Polat, and Franziska Hohlstein. 2021. 'Satisfied or Not? Exploring the Interplay of Individual, Country and International Organization Characteristics for Negotiation Success.' *The Review of International Organizations* 16: 403–29.

Panke, Diana, Sören Stapel, and Anna Starkmann. 2020. *Comparing Regional Organizations: Global Dynamics and Regional Particularities*. Bristol: Bristol University Press.

Perina, Rubén M. 2015. *The Organization of American States as the Advocate and Guardian of Democracy: An Insider's Critical Assessment of Its Role in Promoting and Defending Democracy*. Lanham: University Press of America.

Pevehouse, Jon C. 2005. *Democracy from Above: Regional Organizations and Democratization*. Cambridge: Cambridge University Press.

Pevehouse, Jon C.W., Timothy Nordstrom, Roseanne W. McManus, and Anne Spencer Jamison. 2020. 'Tracking Organizations in the World: The Correlates of War Igo Version 3.0 Datasets.' *Journal of Peace Research* 57: 492–503.

PIF. 2022. *2050 Strategy for the Blue Pacific Continent*. Suva: Pacific Island Forum.

REFERENCES

Plantey, Alain. 2007. *International Negotiation in the Twenty-First Century*. New York: Routledge.

Pouliot, Vincent. 2016. *International Pecking Orders: The Politics and Practice of Multilateral Diplomacy*. New York: Cambridge University Press.

Pouliot, Vincent. 2017. 'Against Authority: The Heavy Weight of International Hierarchy.' In *Hierarchies in World Politics*, ed. Ayşe Zarakol. Cambridge: Cambridge University Press. 115–33.

Pourchot, Georgeta. 2011. 'The OSCE: A Pan-European Society in the Making?'. *Journal of European Integration* 33: 179–95.

Pratt, Tyler. 2023. 'Value Differentiation, Policy Change and Cooperation in International Regime Complexes.' *Review of International Political Economy* 30: 2206–32.

PRS Group, The. 2007. 'Politics.' *The PRS Group/International Country Risk Guide*, 01/10/2007.

Putnam, Robert. 1988. 'Diplomacy and Domestic Politics. The Logic of Two-Level Games.' *International Organization* 42: 427–60.

Qatar News Agency. 2007. 'OSCE Countries Meet Overshadowed by US–Russia Crisis.' *Qatar News Agency*. https://advance.lexis.com/document/?pdmfid=1519360&crid=ce261488-f186-4810-a74b-9bb34dea80d8&pddocfullpath=%2Fshared%2Fdocument%2Fnews%2Furn%3AcontentItem%3A4R7S-KBT0-TWNX-009P-00000-00&pdcontentcomponentid=280798&pdteaserkey=sr7&pditab=allpods&ecomp=hc-yk&earg=sr7&prid=6064b708-b697-4c15-ae91-f819513436eb [last accessed 15 October 2024].

Ramanzini Júnior, Haroldo, and Bruno T. Luciano. 2020. 'Regionalism in the Global South: Mercosur and ECOWAS in Trade and Democracy Protection.' *Third World Quarterly* 41: 1498–517.

Reiners, Wulf, and Funda Tekin. 2020. 'Taking Refuge in Leadership? Facilitators and Constraints of Germany's Influence in Eu Migration Policy and Eu-Turkey Affairs During the Refugee Crisis (2015–2016).' *German Politics* 29: 115–30.

Reisdoerfer, Bruna, and Marc Castillo. 2022. 'The Suspension of Venezuela from Mercosur: Economic and Political Impacts for Brazil.' *Business and Public Administration Studies* 16: 27–34.

Reuters. 2017. 'Mercosur Suspends Venezuela, Urges Immediate Transition.' *Reuters*, 06/08/2017.

Ribeiro, Clarissa C.N. 2022. *Overlapping Regional Organizations in South America and Africa: Coexistence through Political Crises.* Cham: Springer.

Ribeiro Hoffmann, Andrea. 2019. 'Negotiating Normative Premises in Democracy Promotion: Venezuela and the Inter-American Democratic Charter.' *Democratization* 26: 815–31.

Ribeiro Hoffmann, Andrea. 2020. 'Mercosur between Resilience and Disintegration.' In *Regionalism under Stress: Europe and Latin America in Comparative Perspective*, eds. Detlef Nolte and Brigitte Weiffen. London: Routledge.

Risse, Thomas. 2000. '"Let's Argue!": Communicative Action in World Politics.' *International Organization* 54: 1–39.

Risse, Thomas, and Mareike Kleine. 2010. 'Deliberation in Negotiations.' *Journal of European Public Policy* 17: 708–26.

Risse, Thomas, Stephen C. Ropp, and Kathryn Sikkink. 2013. *The Persistent Power of Human Rights: From Commitment to Compliance.* Cambridge: Cambridge University Press.

Risse-Kappen, Thomas. 1995. 'Democratic Peace – Warlike Democracies? A Social Constructivist Interpretation of the Liberal Argument.' *European Journal of International Relations*, Special Issue 1. 489–515.

Rittberger, Volker, Bernhard Zangl, Andreas Kruck, and Hylke Dijkstra. 2019. *International Organization.* London: Macmillan.

Romano, Angela. 2009. 'Détente, Entente, or Linkage? The Helsinki Conference on Security and Cooperation in Europe in U.S. Relations with the Soviet Union.' *Diplomatic History* 33: 703–22.

Rosamond, Ben. 2016. 'Brexit and the Problem of European Disintegration.' *Journal of Contemporary European Research* 12. https://doi.org/10.30950/jcer.v12i4.807.

Rosamond, Ben. 2019. 'Theorising the EU in Crisis: De-Europeanisation as Disintegration.' *Global Discourse* 9: 31–44.

Rudall, Jason. 2018. 'Certain Activities Carried out by Nicaragua in the Border Area (Costa Rica V. Nicaragua).' *American Journal of International Law* 112: 288–94.

REFERENCES

Russett, Bruce M. 1995. 'The Democratic Peace: And Yet It Moves.' *International Security* 19: 164–184.

Russo, Alessandra, and Edward Stoddard. 2018. 'Why Do Authoritarian Leaders Do Regionalism? Ontological Security and Eurasian Regional Cooperation.' *The International Spectator* 53: 20–37.

Sampson, Thomas. 2017. 'Brexit: The Economics of International Disintegration.' *Journal of Economic Perspectives* 31: 163–84.

San Martim Portes, Alexandre. 2017. 'Regime Effectiveness and Democracy Protection: The Responses of Mercosur to the Impeachment Processes in Paraguay and Brazil.' *Conjuntura Austral* 8: 58–70.

Sandole, Dennis J.D. 2007. *Peace and Security in the Postmodern World: The OSCE and Conflict Resolution*. London: Routledge.

Schleich, Anne-Marie. 2021. 'End of Pacific Regionalism?'. *RSIS Commentaries* 037–21.

Schmidt, Averell. 2024. 'Treaty Withdrawal and the Development of International Law.' *The Review of International Organizations*: 1–24.

Schmidtke, Henning. 2019. 'Elite Legitimation and Delegitimation of International Organizations in the Media: Patterns and Explanations.' *The Review of International Organizations* 14: 633–59.

Schmidtke, Henning, and Tobias Lenz. 2023. 'Expanding or Defending Legitimacy? Why International Organizations Intensify Self-Legitimation.' *The Review of International Organizations* 2023.

Schuessler, John M., and Joshua R. Shifrinson. 2019. 'The Shadow of Exit from NATO.' *Strategic Studies Quarterly* 13: 38–51.

Schuette, Leonard August. 2021. 'Why Nato Survived Trump: The Neglected Role of Secretary-General Stoltenberg.' *International Affairs* 97: 1863–81.

Schuette, Leonard, and Hylke Dijkstra. 2023. 'The Show Must Go On: The EU's Quest to Sustain Multilateral Institutions since 2016.' *Journal of Common Market Studies* 61: 1318–36.

Shi, Mingtao. 2018. 'State Withdrawal from International Institutions: Changing Social Relations within Divergent Institutions.' *International Politics* 55: 221–41.

Siman, Tainá. 2023. 'Non-Democracy Tolerance: Venezuela in Mercosur and Hungary in the European Union.' *Regions and Cohesion* 13: 105–18.

Slapin, Jonathan B. 2008. 'Bargaining Power at Europe's Intergovernmental Conferences: Testing Institutional and Intergovernmental Theories.' *International Organization* 62: 131–62.

Slocum, Nikki, and Luk van Langenhove. 2005. 'Identity and Regional Integration.' In *Global Politics of Regionalism: Theory and Practice*, eds. Mary Farrell, Björn Hettne and Luk van Langenhove. London: Pluto. 137–51.

SNS. 2017. 'Another Chance to Right a Wrong in Azerbaijan.' *States News Service*, 16/11/2017.

Söderbaum, Fredrik. 1996. *Handbook of Regional Organizations in Africa*. Uppsala: Nordiska Afrikainstitutet.

Söderbaum, Fredrik. 2016. *Rethinking Regionalism*. London: Palgrave.

Söderbaum, Fredrik, Kilian Spandler, and Agnese Pacciardi. 2021. *Contestations of the Liberal International Order: A Populist Script of Regional Cooperation*. Cambridge: Cambridge University Press.

Sommerer, Thomas, Hans Agné, Fariborz Zelli, and Bart Bes. 2022. *Global Legitimacy Crises: Decline and Revival in Multilateral Governance*. Oxford: Oxford University Press.

Soyaltin-Colella, Digdem. 2020. '(Un)Democratic Change and Use of Social Sanctions for Domestic Politics: Council of Europe Monitoring in Turkey.' *International Political Science Review* 42: 484–500.

Spandler, Kilian. 2018. 'Regional Standards of Membership and Enlargement in the EU and ASEAN.' *Asia Europe Journal* 16: 183–98.

Spandler, Kilian. 2019. *Regional Organizations in International Society: ASEAN, the EU and the Politics of Normative Arguing*. Cham: Springer.

Spandler, Kilian, and Frederik Söderbaum. 2023. 'Populist (De) Legitimation of International Organizations.' *International Affairs* 99: 1023–41.

Sperling, James, and Mark Webber. 2019. 'Trump's Foreign Policy and Nato: Exit and Voice.' *Review of International Studies* 45: 511–26.

REFERENCES

Stapel, Sören. 2022. *Regional Organizations and Democracy, Human Rights, and the Rule of Law: The African Union, Organization of Americas States, and the Diffusion of Institutions.* Houndmills: Palgrave Macmillan.

Steiner, Ludwig. 1982. 'Memorandum on the Situation in Turkey'. *Parliamentary Assembly of the Council of Europe.* https://search.coe.int/archives?i=09000016807a96a0 [last accessed 23 September 2024].

Stephen, Matthew D. 2021. 'China's New Multilateral Institutions: A Framework and Research Agenda.' *International Studies Review* 23: 807–34.

Stewart, Emma J. 2008. 'Restoring EU–OSCE Cooperation for Pan-European Conflict Prevention.' *Contemporary Security Policy* 29: 266–84.

Stoddard, Edward. 2017. 'Authoritarian Regimes in Democratic Regional Organisations? Exploring Regional Dimensions of Authoritarianism in an Increasingly Democratic West Africa.' *Journal of Contemporary African Studies* 35: 469–86.

Strait Times, The. 2020. 'Micronesian Leaders Threaten to Leave Pacific Forum.' *The Strait Times*, 05/10/2020.

Striebinger, Kai. 2012. 'When Pigs Fly: ECOWAS and the Protection of Constitutional Order in Events of Coups D'état.' In *Roads to Regionalism: Genesis, Design, and Effects of Regional Organizations*, eds. Tanja Börzel, Lukas Goltermann, Mathis Lohaus and Kai Striebinger. Farnham: Ashgate. 179–96.

Sunday Trust. 2022. 'How Other Countries "Shortchange" Nigeria in ECOWAS.' *Sunday Trust.* https://dailytrust.com/how-other-countries-shortchange-nigeria-in-ecowas/ [last accessed 9 October 2024].

Suzuki, Sanae. 2020a. 'Exploring the Roles of the AU and ECOWAS in West African Conflicts.' *South African Journal of International Affairs* 27: 173–91.

Suzuki, Sanae. 2020b. 'Increasing Ownership for Intervention in ECOWAS.' *African Security Review* 29: 364–75.

Szucs, Rebecca. 2014. 'A Democracy's Poor Performance: The Impeachment of Paraguayan President Fernando Lugo.' *George Washington International Law Review* 46: 409–36.

Tajikistan Newsline. 2021. 'Lack of Active Work of the Eaeu Countries Causes Imbalance of Exports and Imports in 2020.' *Tajikistan Newsline*, 23/02/2021.

Tallberg, Jonas, Thomas Sommerer, and Theresa Squatrito. 2016. 'Democratic Memberships in International Organizations: Sources of Institutional Design.' *The Review of International Organizations* 11: 59–87.

Tarte, Sandra. 2014. 'Regionalism and Changing Regional Order in the Pacific Islands.' *Asia & the Pacific Policy Studies* 1: 312–24.

Taylor, Scott. 2016. 'Region-Building in Southern Africa.' In *Region-Building in Africa: Political and Economic Challenges*, eds. Daniel H. Levine and Dawn Nagar. Houndsmill: Palgrave. 157–74.

Thai Examiner. 2024. 'Rising World Tensions and Potential South China Sea Conflict Being Dealt with at Laos Asian Summit.' *Thai Examiner*, 27/07/2024.

Thai News Service. 2018. 'Colombia/United States: Colombia Announces Withdrawal from South American Bloc Conceived to Counter US.' *Thai News Service*, 29/08/2018.

Thomas, Daniel C. 2017. 'Beyond Identity: Membership Norms and Regional Organization.' *European Journal of International Relations* 23: 217–40.

Thorhallsson, Baldur, ed. 2018. *Small State and Shelter Theory: Iceland's External Affairs*. London: Routledge.

Trend Daily News. 2018. 'Council of Europe Warns of Russia's Possible Withdrawal.' *Trend Daily News*, 09/11/2018.

Treshchenkov, E. 2019. 'Resilience in Discourses of the European Union and International Organizations.' *International Organisations Research Journal* 14: 55–75.

United News of India. 2018. 'Russia May Exit Council of Europe Amid Growing Crisis in Relations: Lower House Speaker.' *United News of India*, 13/10/2018.

UPI. 2017. 'Venezuela to Withdraw from "Shameful" OAS.' *United Press International*, 27/04/2017.

Vines, Alex. 2013. 'A Decade of African Peace and Security Architecture.' *International Affairs* 89: 89–109.

REFERENCES

Vinokurov, Evgeny. 2017. 'Eurasian Economic Union: Current State and Preliminary Results.' *Russian Journal of Economics* 3: 54–70.

Vinokurov, Evgeny, and Alexander Libman. 2017. *Re-Evaluating Regional Organizations: Behind the Smokescreen of Official Mandates*. Houndmills: Palgrave Macmillan.

VOA News. 2017. 'Mercosur Suspends Venezuela over Unrest, Repression.' *Voice of America News*, 05/08/2017.

Voice of America. 2016. 'Venezuela Decries Mercosur "Coup" after Trade Bloc Suspension.' *Voice of America*, 02/12/2016.

von Billerbeck, Sarah. 2020. '"Mirror, Mirror on the Wall": Self-Legitimation by International Organizations.' *International Studies Quarterly* 64: 207–19.

von Billerbeck, Sarah. 2023. 'Organizational Narratives and Self-Legitimation in International Organizations.' *International Affairs* 99: 963–81.

von Borzyskowski, Inken, and Felicity Vabulas. 2019a. 'Credible Commitments? Explaining IGO Suspensions to Sanction Political Backsliding.' *International Studies Quarterly* 63: 139–52.

von Borzyskowski, Inken, and Felicity Vabulas. 2019b. 'Hello, Goodbye: When Do States Withdraw from International Organizations?'. *The Review of International Organizations* 14: 335–66.

von Borzyskowski, Inken, and Felicity Vabulas. 2022. 'On IGO Withdrawal by States Vs Leaders, and Exogenous Measures for Inference.' *Global Perspectives* 4: 1–18.

von Borzyskowski, Inken, and Felicity Vabulas. 2023. 'When Do Withdrawal Threats Achieve Reform in International Organizations?'. *Global Perspectives* 4: 1–18.

von Borzyskowski, Inken, and Felicity Vabulas. 2024a. 'Public Support for Withdrawal from International Organizations: Experimental Evidence from the US.' *The Review of International Organizations*. https://doi.org/10.1007/s11558-024-09539-2.

von Borzyskowski, Inken, and Felicity Vabulas. 2024b. 'When Do Member State Withdrawals Lead to the Death of International Organizations?'. *European Journal of International Relations*. https://doi.org/10.1177/13540661241256951.

von Borzyskowski, Inken, and Felicity Vabulas. 2025. *Exit from International Organizations: Costly Negotiation for Institutional Change*. Cambridge: Cambridge University Press.

Wagner, Wolfgang, and Rosanne Anholt. 2016. 'Resilience as the EU Global Strategy's New Leitmotif: Pragmatic, Problematic or Promising?'. *Contemporary Security Policy* 37: 414–30.

Walter, Stefanie. 2021. 'Brexit Domino? The Political Contagion Effects of Voter-Endorsed Withdrawals from International Institutions.' *Comparative Political Studies* 54: 2382–415.

Warkotsch, Alexander. 2007. ' International Socialization in Difficult Environments: The Organisation for Security and Cooperation in Europe in Central Asia.' *Democratisation* 14: 491–508.

Wästfelt, Margit, Pibernik, Tania. 2017. 'Central European Initiative: 25 Years for Central and Southeastern Europe.' In *Die EU-Strategie Für Den Donauraum Auf Dem Prüfstand: Erfahrungen Und Perspektiven*, eds. Ellen Griessler, Christina Bos, and Christopher Walsch. Wien: Nomos. 231–42.

Weiffen, Brigitte. 2017. 'Institutional Overlap and Responses to Political Crises in South America.' In *Power Dynamics and Regional Security in Latin America*, eds. Marcial A.G. Suarez, Rafael Duarte Villa and Brigitte Weiffen. London: Palgrave Macmillan UK. 173–97.

Weiffen, Brigitte, Leslie Wehner, and Detlef Nolte. 2013. 'Overlapping Regional Security Institutions in South America: The Case of OAS and UNASUR.' *International Area Studies Review* 16: 370–89.

West Australian, The. 2023. 'Wong Backing Waqa as PIF Secretary General.' *The West Australian*, 06/03/2023.

Wiener, Antje. 2018. *Contestation and Constitution of Norms in Global International Relations*. Cambridge: Cambridge University Press.

World News Digest. 1980. 'Human Rights Resolution Passed.' *Facts on File World News Digest*, 05/12/1980.

WTPS. 2008. 'Let's Withdraw: Russia Is Preparing to Suspend Its OSCE Membership.' *What the Papers Say Weekly Review (Russia)*, 11/08/2008.

Xinhua. 2007. 'South Pacific Countries Vow to Continue Regional Cooperation.' *Xinhua General News Service*, 16/10/2007.

REFERENCES

Yaya, Bappah H. 2014. 'ECOWAS and the Promotion of Democratic Governance in West Africa.' *Journal of International Relations and Foreign Policy* 2: 85–102.

Zartman, I. William, and Jeffrey Z. Rubin, eds. 2009. *Power and Negotiation*. Michigan: University of Michigan Press.

Zimmermann, Lisbeth, Nicole Deitelhoff, Antonio Arcudi, and Anton Peez. 2023. *International Norm Disputes: The Link between Contestation and Norm Robustness*. Oxford: Oxford University Press.

Index

A
Africa 2, 8, 26, 38, 110
African subregions 25
African Union (AU) 4, 25, 108
Americas 2, 8, 24–25, 38, 70, 110
Andean Community (ANDEAN) 1, 4, 8, 19, 40, 98–99
Asia 2, 8, 40
Asia Cooperation Dialogue (ACD) 36
authoritarian leaders *see* autocracy
autocracy 2, 4, 9–10, 17, 54, 57, 60, 78–80, 85–86, 88, 96
autocratic states *see* autocracy

B
bargaining 47–50, 61, 67, 69
blame-shifting 13
bureaucracy 29–30, 48, 97

C
Central European Initiative (CEI) 3, 81
Community of Latin American and Caribbean States (CELAC) 36
community organization 2–3, 5, 7, 16, 19, 27, 56, 88, 105
comparative regionalism 6, 14
compliance 13, 37
contagion effect 61, 63
contestation 2–3, 5–7, 10–15, 29–30, 32, 35, 42, 44, 54, 84–85, 88, 92–95, 97, 103–106
Council of Europe (CoE) 19, 21, 75

D
decision-making 10–11, 18–19, 47–49, 51, 53, 56–57, 60, 70, 72, 75, 79, 87, 95, 101, 104–105
delegation 18, 21–22, 33, 61–62, 74–75, 91
democracy 2, 4, 6–7, 9–13, 17, 24, 35, 53–55, 57, 60, 66, 68–71, 73–74, 78–80, 82–88, 90, 96, 99, 104–105
democracy norms *see* democracy
democratic *see* democracy
democratic member states *see* democracy
democratization *see* democracy
development 17, 57, 66, 73, 80, 94, 101
diffuse support 6–7, 9–13, 44, 47, 51–55, 60, 64, 77–81, 83–88, 93–96, 104–105
disintegration 29, 94, 97
dissatisfaction 3, 5, 7–9, 11–12, 16, 19–28, 32, 36, 38, 42–44, 46–47, 51–52, 60, 68, 70, 72–73, 76–77, 81, 86–87, 95, 98, 104–105
domestic politics 79

E
Eastern African Community (EAC) 1, 4, 36, 40, 100–101
Easton's systems theory 6, 8–9, 11, 13, 43–47, 52, 54, 58–59, 64, 85, 88, 90, 94, 96
Economic Community of West African States (ECOWAS) 5, 19
economic competencies 63, 75
economic indicators 59
economic terms 62
economies of scale 103
economy and trade 18, 57
effectiveness 3, 5, 11, 13, 15, 30, 32, 93–94, 105
environment 17–18, 25, 46, 49, 52, 56–57, 59
Eurasian Economic Union (EAEU) 38, 40, 69–70, 75–77, 79, 84, 101

INDEX

Europe 2, 8, 21, 38, 68
European Court of Human Rights 21
European Union (EU) 1, 4, 31
exit 3–4, 11, 13, 28–38, 61, 63, 67, 70, 75–79, 81, 84, 86, 91–100, 103, 105
exit threat 2–14, 16, 19–21, 23, 28–45, 47, 49–58, 60–64, 66–72, 74–81, 83–88, 90–101, 103–105

G

geopolitics 27, 62–63, 76
global governance 11, 14
good governance 18, 79
gross domestic product (GDP) 12, 59, 63
Gulf Cooperation Council (GCC) 8

H

health 18, 25, 57
human rights 18–19, 21, 25, 52, 68, 70–71, 73–74, 80

I

institutional design 9, 14–15, 45, 47, 61, 75, 86, 95, 101
institutional reform 101, 103
integration initiatives 70
integration project 22, 31
Inter-American Commission on Human Rights (IACHR) 70
International Labour Organization (ILO) 50
international order 14, 29

L

Latin America 24, 36
legalization 19, 91–92
legitimacy 3, 5–6, 11, 14–15, 24, 32, 44–45, 51, 53–55, 84–86, 94, 97, 104–105
legitimate *see* legitimacy

Liberal International Order (LIO) 29
liberal script 84

M

majority rule 10, 50–51, 59–61, 72, 77, 87, 96
majority voting 6, 12, 19, 50, 74, 86, 95–96
mandates 18, 25, 46, 75
membership 2–5, 12, 17–19, 23, 28, 30, 32–33, 40, 52, 54, 56, 60–63, 68, 70, 75–76, 81–85, 88, 92, 94, 96, 98–100, 103–104
membership criterion 2, 5, 17, 61
migration 12, 18

N

nationalism 7
norm contestation 13
North Atlantic Free Trade Agreement (NAFTA) 7, 40, 84, 99
North Atlantic Treaty Organization (NATO) 2–5, 7, 12, 18, 32–33, 40, 50, 81, 84, 94

O

Organization of American States (OAS) 5, 19, 24, 25, 38, 40, 50, 70–74, 76–77, 82, 84, 99–100
Office for Democratic Institutions and Human Rights (ODIHR) 68

P

Pacific Islands Forum (PIF) 4, 8, 34, 38, 40, 80, 84, 94, 98, 100–103
Peace and Security Council (PSC) 25–26
policy competencies 2, 5–6, 10, 12, 18, 27, 49, 50, 57, 59, 75–76, 87, 90
policy output 6, 9, 18, 20, 46, 67, 74, 77, 105

policy scope 9–11, 50–51, 54, 59, 63, 72, 75, 77, 86–88, 90, 95–96, 105
policy making 26, 49, 51, 55, 86
pooling 18, 49, 59, 61, 72, 95
populism 7
primary law 5, 61

R

regime complexity 61–62
regime type 19, 59
regional court 62, 91
regional governance 2, 5, 15, 18
regional hegemon 61–62, 66
Regional Organizations' Competencies (ROCO) 2.0 dataset *see* ROCO dataset
regionalism 6, 14, 40
resilience 6, 12, 14, 32, 87, 94–95, 97, 103, 105–106
ROCO dataset 8, 29, 36, 58–63

S

security 12, 18, 25, 31, 40, 50, 57, 59, 62–63, 66, 68–69, 75–76, 85
socialization 6–7, 9–10, 12, 52, 78–88, 96
South Pacific Forum (SPC) 34, 38, 40
specific support 6–7, 9–13, 45, 47, 49–51, 54, 56–57, 59, 64, 66–67, 70, 72, 74–78, 86–88, 94–96, 104

U

UN Security Council (UNSC) 25
Union of South American Nations (UNASUR) 8, 40, 98
United Nations General Assembly (UNGA) 18
United Nations (UN) 18, 50

W

withdrawal *see* exit

www.ingramcontent.com/pod-product-compliance
Lightning Source LLC
Chambersburg PA
CBHW071708020426
42333CB00017B/2190